*This book is dedicated to April Renee (Green) Smock,
our daughter and a middle school teacher
at The Athenian School in Danville, California.
April is the teacher I would like
to have been and the emerging educational leader
that this book recognizes and celebrates.*

Acknowledgments

Morgan Dale Lambert is my friend, my inspiration, and my husband. His support and insights make the roles that I play possible and the work I do credible. I thank him for his editorial work on this book and the many conversations during which the ideas took form. He played a particularly vital role in conceptualizing the role of the school district in building leadership capacity. I also want to deeply thank the Administrative Credential students and faculty at California State University-Hayward (CSUH) and teacher leaders in the CSUH Professional Development Schools for helping me understand the vitality and substance of building leadership capacity.

BUILDING LEADERSHIP CAPACITY IN SCHOOLS

❧ Linda Lambert ❧

Association for Supervision and Curriculum Development

Alexandria, Virginia USA

Association for Supervision and Curriculum Development
1703 N. Beauregard St. • Alexandria, VA 22311-1714 USA
Telephone: 1-800-933-2723 or 703-578-9600
Web site: http://www.ascd.org • E-mail: member@ascd.org

Gene R. Carter, *Executive Director*
Michelle Terry, *Associate Executive Director, Program Development*
Nancy Modrak, *Director, Publishing*
John O'Neil, *Acquisitions Director*
Mark Goldberg, *Development Editor*
Julie Houtz, *Managing Editor of Books*
Carolyn R. Pool, *Associate Editor*
Kathleen Larson Florio, *Copy Editor*
Charles D. Halverson, *Project Assistant*

Gary Bloom, *Director, Design and Production Services*
Karen Monaco, *Senior Designer*
Tracey A. Smith, *Production Manager*
Dina Murray, *Production Coordinator*
John Franklin, *Production Coordinator*
Cynthia Stock, *Desktop Publisher*
Hilary Cumberton, *Indexer, M. L. Coughlin Editorial Services*

Printed in the United States of America.

November 1998 member book (pc). ASCD Premium, Comprehensive, and Regular members periodically receive ASCD books as part of their membership benefits. No. FY99-2.

ASCD Stock No. 198058
ASCD member price: $10.95; nonmember price: $13.95

Library of Congress Cataloging-in-Publication Data

Lambert, Linda, 1939–
    Building leadership capacity in schools / Linda Lambert.
    p. cm.
    Includes bibliographical references.
    ISBN 0-87120-307-3 (pbk.)
    1. Educational leadership—United States. 2. Teacher participation in administration—United States. 3. Community and school—United States. 4. Educational change—United States I. Association for Supervision and Curriculum Development. II. Title.
    LB2805 .L26 1998
    371.2'00973—ddc21
                                                98-40095
                                                     CIP

05 04 03 02 01 00 99 98   10 9 8 7 6 5 4 3 2 1

BUILDING LEADERSHIP CAPACITY IN SCHOOLS

WHAT IS LEADERSHIP CAPACITY?

WHEN JENNIFER FIELDING DECIDED TO APPLY FOR A TRANSFER to Belvedere Middle School,[1] it was with good reason. With almost three years of teaching under her belt, she was beginning to feel a new sense of confidence. Not that she knew all there was to know about teaching—far from it—but she was ready to be more involved in work beyond the classroom. She found herself more concerned with children in other classrooms and families in the surrounding community, and she felt uncomfortable with the restrictions on the "talk" in the faculty room at her current school.

This year, she had participated in the district curriculum committee and attended a middle school networking conversation. There she had met a few teachers from Belvedere Middle School. She was impressed. They talked with clear excitement about what was going on at Belvedere; they seemed to share an understanding about what they were trying to accomplish. Some of the reforms that she was

---

[1]Belvedere Middle School, Arabesque Elementary School, Capricorn High School, and Fairview High School (and the names of staff members) are all pseudonyms.

reading about were beyond the talking stage at Belvedere. By mid-April, she had made her decision. When an opening in the social studies/language arts core occurred, she applied for a transfer.

In late August and September she was beginning to teach in her new assignment at Belvedere. She was paired with a school mentor, Gary, a veteran teacher of eight years. The orientation and support he provided were extremely helpful. Gary shared lessons, answered questions, and introduced her to other staff and a few active parents. Yet in the hallways and faculty room she detected a familiar tone: cynicism, misplaced humor, even anger about the school's plans for improvement. "What happened?" Jennifer earnestly asked. "This isn't quite what I expected."

Gary replied solemnly, "Our principal left."

Gary might also have answered, "Two key teachers left," "We had a change of superintendents," "There was an election and we got a new board majority," "We reached the implementation stages, but a few resistant teachers killed the central ideas or weakened them beyond recognition," "The grant money ran out," "The new state mandates have changed the direction of reform."

This is not an unfamiliar story. In many schools, momentum, energy, and growing commitment begin to form around some key improvement ideas; then a change in key personnel or mandated directions derails the effort. It is no wonder that veteran educators become discouraged and cynical and that new teachers leave the profession. How many times can you ride this merry-go-round before deciding to jump off?

Ask any number of strong and seemingly effective principals what happened in the school that they just left. Many will reluctantly and sadly tell you, "The school went right back to the way it was before." Well, that's not quite accurate. Schools and people never entirely return to the way they were before. Each time they rebound from a failed effort, they are more deeply disappointed, more cynical, more wounded. Each time, improvement in that school becomes more difficult to achieve. As long as improvement is dependent on a single person or a few people or outside directions and forces, it will fail. Schools, and the people in them, have a tendency to depend too much on a strong principal or other authority for direction and guidance.

Any number of responses could now occur at Belvedere Middle School. A few key teachers could refuse to let their progress slip away and decide to take hold of the reins of reform and pull things back together. The new principal could be strong and wise and able to work with the school to recapture some of its previous momentum. The school could choose to envelop itself in regrets and remorse and let go of cherished innovations. In Chapter 4, you will discover in detail what happened at Belvedere Middle School.

When Jennifer asked her powerful question, "What happened?" several teachers at Belvedere Middle School were enmeshed in self-pity. Those who had been tentative about the reforms were quick to point out how fragile the reforms were; those who had been somewhat resistant felt vindicated. Hadn't they warned that the school was moving too fast, with too many changes? Accustomed to looking to someone with formal authority to lead the way, the teacher analysts failed to recognize that leadership lies within the school, not just in the chair of the principal; that the school must build its own leadership capacity if it is to stay afloat, assume internal responsibility for reform, and maintain a momentum for self-renewal.

When I refer to building "leadership capacity," I mean broad-based, skillful involvement in the work of leadership. To establish enduring leadership capacity at Belvedere, at least two critical conditions would be necessary:

1. The school would need a significant number of skillful teacher-leaders who understand the shared vision of the school and the full scope of the work underway, and who are able to carry them out.

These teachers ideally would be involved in the selection and induction of the new principal.

2. School staff would need to be committed to the central work of self-renewing schools. This work involves reflection, inquiry, conversations and focused action—professional behaviors that are an integral part of daily work.

These conditions speak to two critical dimensions that we will explore in depth: (1) breadth of involvement and (2) understandings and skillfulness of those involved. Understandings and skillfulness involve more than knowledge of an innovation (e.g., a new curriculum program, schedule, or structural arrangement). The skillfulness addressed here consists of those skills of leadership that allow adults to capture the imagination of their colleagues, and that enable them to negotiate real changes in their own schools and to tackle the inevitable conflicts that arise from such courageous undertakings.

This book will explore in detail the meaning of and the strategies involved in building leadership capacity in schools. Before I address the concept of leadership capacity in detail, however, it is important to say more about what I mean by "leadership." "Despite thousands of empirical studies yielding hundreds of definitions of leadership, there is still no consensus about it" (Evans, 1996, p. 116). One of the advantages about having no consensus on such a public idea as leadership is that the concept is still open for discussion.

What Is Leadership?

Most of us probably think of a particular person or set of behaviors when we think of leadership. When we use the word "leadership," the next sentence often suggests what the principal, superintendent, or president did or did not do. "We have strong leadership in the school." "We have weak leadership in this school, and we are clearly not going to achieve our goals." "We need a change of leadership!" Each of these assertions refers to the principal. We generally consider leadership to be synonymous with a person in a position of formal authority.

When we equate the powerful concept of leadership with the behaviors of one person, we are limiting the achievement of broad-based participation by a community or a society. School leadership needs to be a broad concept that is separated from person, role, and a discrete set of individual behaviors. It needs to be embedded in the school community as a whole. Such a broadening of the concept of leadership suggests shared responsibility for a shared purpose of community.

When we equate "leadership" with "leader," we are immersed in "trait theory": If only a leader possessed these certain traits, we would have good leadership. This tendency has caused those who might have rolled up their sleeves and pitched in to help to abstain from the work of leadership, thereby abdicating both their responsibilities and their opportunities. Although leaders do perform acts of leadership, a separation of the concepts can allow us to reconceptualize leadership itself.

Leadership needs to speak to a group broader than the individual leaders. This breadth can become more evident if we consider the connections or learning processes among individuals in a school community. This concept that I call "leadership" is broader than the sum total of its "leaders," for it also involves an energy flow or synergy generated by those who choose to lead. Sometimes we think of our reactions to an energized environment as being caught up in the excitement and stimulation of an idea or a movement. It is this wave of energy and purpose that engages and pulls others into the work of leadership. This is what it is like to have a group of "leaders," including, of course, the principal, engaged in improving a school.

The key notion in this definition is that leadership is about learning together, and constructing meaning and knowledge collectively and collaboratively. It involves opportunities to surface and mediate perceptions, values, beliefs, information, and assumptions through continuing conversations; to inquire about and generate ideas together; to seek to reflect upon and make sense of work in the light of shared beliefs and new information; and to create actions that grow out of these new understandings. Such is the core of leadership.

When the Fairview High School staff and community, working together, identified and clarified their values, beliefs, assumptions, and perceptions about what they wanted children to know and be able to do, an important next step was to discover which of these values and expectations were now being achieved. Such a discovery required that the staff and community members inquire into their own practice. What information do we have? What information do we need?[2] The problems to be solved rested in the discrepancies: Is there a gap between our current practice and achievements and what we want children to *be able* to know and *be able* to do?

These conversations clarified and framed the school's plans and actions for improvement. Further, these conversations also identified responsibilities and strategies for implementation and for continuous feedback that could be understood by the entire school community—not just the principal or the principal and one or two teachers. This is a difficult undertaking. Throughout this book, I will describe the leadership dispositions, understandings, and skills that are essential if schools are to tackle such elegant and demanding work.

Using the Fairview High example above, let's look more closely at the key *reciprocal learning processes* that engaged this school community in the work of leadership, enabling the community to renew itself. (The stories told in Chapters 3 through 5 describe some of the ways in which these processes are carried out in schools.)

1. Surface, clarify, and define community values, beliefs, assumptions, perceptions, and experiences. Fairview chose to use this process as a means to discover what they valued about students' learning

---

[2]For a thorough discussion of the inquiry process, see Sagor, 1992; Glickman, 1993; Calhoun, 1994.

(what students should know and be able to do). Such an effort requires many small and informal conversations as well as large-group work, in which staff surface and consider their personal schemas (what they already believe, think, and know). Fundamentally, learning is about clarifying and altering these personal schemas as shared beliefs and purpose are created and evolve.

2. *Inquire into practice.* Discover or generate information (data) that could point to whether or not—and how well—students are learning in the desired ways. Fairveiw staff looked at student work, disaggregated test and participation data (e.g., attendance, suspensions), and a community profile. They formed collaborative action research teams to help them understand whether all students were learning equitably.

3. *Construct meaning and knowledge* by comparing beliefs and expectations with the results of the inquiry. The "problem(s)" or issues to be considered reside in this discrepancy. In these conversations (involving both large and small groups), the Fairview community made sense of what was occurring with student learning in their school and more clearly identified the problems to be solved. They ultimately realized that three areas constituted major needs: improvement of student writing, understanding of science concepts, and development of skills in cooperative work.

4. *Frame action and develop implementation plans* on the basis of the various conversations. At Fairview, the school staff, with active leadership from many teachers and the principal, decided to have a schoolwide research paper, to schedule field trips that emphasized the same environmental concepts, to teach all students the skills of cooperative learning, and to expand student involvement in decision making. The action plan included strategies for implementation, continuous feedback from inside and outside the school, and provisions for shared responsibility. This is where the rubber meets the road, so to speak; this is where broad-based responsibility for leadership work can be most critical.

These processes are part of a repertoire of continuous learning interactions. Staff need to continually tie their work conversations to their shared purpose: "Now, what is it that we are trying to do here?" "Why is that?" Altering personal and collective schemas requires revisiting and reinterpreting ideas many times—in hallway conversations, informal small-group dialogue, lively faculty discussions, and quiet personal reflection as well as structured meetings.

All of the learning must be embedded in a trusting environment in which relationships form a safety net of support and positive challenge (like a net under a high-wire walker). Especially in the beginning, people are taking risks. Because these processes occur among participants in a school community, it means that people are *in relationship with one another*. To be in authentic relationship means that we provide long-term support for one another, challenging one another to improve and to question our current perceptions, and to learn together. Attention to relationship is critical, for, just as in the classroom, "process is content" (Costa & Garmston, 1994).

Not all learning processes constitute leadership. To be "leadership," these processes must enable participants *to learn themselves toward a shared sense of purpose*—a purpose made real by the collaboration of committed adults. Leadership has direction and momentum, and it negotiates tough passages. It is this type of leadership we are seeking to build—the capacity to collectively learn ourselves toward purposeful action so that a school community can keep moving when current leaders leave—whether the leaders are two teachers, a principal, or a powerful parent.

Key Assumptions

Five assumptions form the conceptual framework for building leadership capacity:

1. Leadership is not trait theory; leadership and leader are not the same. *Leadership* can mean (and does mean in this context) the

reciprocal learning processes that enable participants to construct and negotiate meanings leading to a shared purpose of schooling.

2. Leadership is about learning that leads to constructive change. Learning is among participants and therefore occurs collectively. Learning has direction toward a shared purpose.

3. Everyone has the potential and right to work as a leader. Leading is skilled and complicated work that *every member of the school community can learn*. Democracy clearly defines the rights of individuals to actively participate in the decisions that affect their lives.

4. Leading is a shared endeavor, the foundation for the democratization of schools. School change is a collective endeavor; therefore, people do this most effectively in the presence of others. The learning journey must be shared; otherwise, shared purpose and action are never achieved.

5. Leadership requires the redistribution of power and authority. Shared learning, purpose, action, and responsibility demand the realignment of power and authority. Districts and principals need to explicitly release authority, and staff need to learn how to enhance personal power and informal authority (for a fuller examination of this notion, see Lambert, Kent, Richert, Collay, & Dietz, 1997, pp. 122–143).

Together, these assumptions advance the ideas that I believe are essential if we are to develop sustainable, self-renewing schools.

CONNECTING CAPACITY
BUILDING WITH LEADERSHIP

WHEN THE PRINCIPAL LEFT BELVEDERE SCHOOL, THE FACULTY and the parents lacked the capacity to sustain its efforts at renewal. The gap left by her leaving was too large and too strategically placed (the things that she did were done only by her). The walls came tumbling down—at least, so it seemed. The reforms begun at Belvedere had created a good foundation for further capacity building: teachers were working together, decisions were being made jointly, a shared vision was emerging—certainly enough for teachers from other schools to notice. Belvedere was at a crossroads, one that was so fragile that those who were unsure wavered. Now would be the time for teachers and the new principal to recall their accomplishments and push forward, to use their leadership skills to further the capacity of the school for self-responsibility—this time with broader-based engagement.

Over the past 20 years, the term "capacity building" has frequently appeared in the education reform literature in the United States, although more so in the 1970s and '90s than in the '80s. Ann Lieberman (personal communication, 1997) points out that it was a very popular term in the '70s and referred to creating the experiences and opportunities for people to learn how to do certain things. In the early '70s, improving schools through capacity building meant that principals would organize the school for improvement, teachers would learn to work in teams, and teachers would talk publicly about what they were doing. Many of the current reform strategies—inquiry, shared leadership, collaboration, collective responsibility—are woven into definitions of capacity building. The driving force in both eras, although not stated explicitly, has been the expansion or thickening of leadership. In the reform climate of the '90s, capacity building has taken on new importance.

Newmann and Wehlage in their 1995 work, *Successful School Restructuring*, firmly link student achievement to the effective work habits of adults:

> The most successful schools were those that used restructuring tools to help them function as professional communities. That is, they found a way to channel staff and student efforts toward a clear, commonly shared purpose for student learning; they created opportunities for teachers to collaborate and help one another achieve the purpose; and teachers in these schools took collective—not just individual—responsibility for student learning. Schools with strong professional communities were better able to offer authentic pedagogy and were more effective in promoting student achievement (p. 3).

The habits and conditions that allow a staff to work well as a unit contribute to a "professional community." Such communities are places in which teachers participate in decision making, have a shared sense of purpose, engage in collaborative work, and accept joint responsibility for the outcomes of their work. These dispositions and skills, as we shall see later, can be understood as leadership skills.

Definitions of capacity building include the usefulness of building an infrastructure of support that is aligned with the work of the school. This infrastructure usually involves the philosophy and mission of a district and school; the process for selecting personnel; resources (time, money, and talent); staff training; work structures; policies; and available outside networks. If a district supports the internal capacity building of a school, it might delegate staff selection, resource allocation, and staff development decisions to the school. Further, the district would work with the school board to develop congruent policies for decentralization and to establish internal and external networks among schools and within the region. Chapter 6 describes these actions in more detail.

Viewing leadership as a collective learning process leads to the recognition that the dispositions, knowledge, and skills of capacity building are the same as those of leadership. Leadership capacity building, then, can be defined as broad-based, skillful participation in the *work of leadership*. This perspective focuses on two critical dimensions of participation—breadth and skillfulness:

• *Broad-based participation* means involving many people—administrators, parents, students, community members, district personnel, university faculty—in the work of leadership. I often refer to staff in discussions of building leadership capacity because they are the center of the effort. However, most schools will add members of the broader school community to their reform effort.

• *Skillful participation* refers to participants' comprehensive understanding of and demonstrated proficiency in the dispositions, knowledge, and skills of leadership.

A Leadership Capacity Matrix

The intersection of these two dimensions creates a dynamic relationship that allows us to describe conditions in schools with different levels of leadership capacity, as shown in the Leadership Capacity Matrix (see Figure 2.1). Each set of descriptors in the matrix addresses the role of the formal leader(s), the flow of information, defined staff roles, relationships among staff, norms, innovation in teaching and learning, and student achievement.

Figure 2.1. Leadership Capacity Matrix

Low skillfulness

Quadrant 1 (Low participation / Low skillfulness)

- Autocratic administration
- Limited (primarily one-way) flow of information
- Codependent, paternal relationships
- Rigidly defined roles
- Norms of compliance
- Lack of innovation in teaching and learning
- Student achievement poor or showing short-term improvement

Quadrant 2 (High participation / Low skillfulness)

- Laissez-faire administration
- Fragmentation and lack of coherence of information and programs
- Norms of individualism
- Undefined roles and responsibilities
- Both excellent and poor classrooms
- "Spotty" innovation
- Student achievement static overall

High participation

Low participation

Quadrant 3 (Low participation / High skillfulness)

- Trained leadership or site-based management team
- Limited uses of schoolwide data, information flow
- Within designated leadership groups
- Polarized staff, pockets of strong resistance
- Designated leaders acting efficiently; others serving in traditional roles
- Pockets of strong innovation and excellent classrooms
- Student achievement static or showing slight improvement

Quadrant 4 (High participation / High skillfulness)

- Broad-based, skillful participation in the work of leadership
- Inquiry-based use of information to inform decisions and practice
- Roles and responsibilities that reflect broad involvement and collaboration
- Reflective practice/innovation as the norm
- High student achievement

High skillfulness

A caveat is necessary here. Whenever complex issues or conditions are divided into neat boxes, a problem results. Conditions are never neatly bound or clearly delineated. As you examine this matrix, keep that caveat in mind, realizing that these are approximations that often overlap and intermingle.

Quadrant 1: Low participation, low skillfulness

In a Quadrant 1 school, the principal often exercises autocratic leadership. The flow of information is one-way—from the principal to the staff (as well as from the superintendent to the principal). Presented information is usually regulatory in nature and requires staff compliance. Relationships are codependent; that is, teachers depend upon the principal for answers and guidance, and the principal depends upon the teachers to validate and reinforce his or her autocratic style. Those staff who would be actively resistant in a more open environment express their resistance in silent, nearly invisible ways (e.g., leaving as soon as school is out, absenteeism, doctor appointments on faculty meeting days). There is little innovation in teaching and learning among teachers. Proposals for new practices come from the top, and compliance is expected. Although short-term student achievement may rise, the increase is not sustainable, and student achievement will quickly return to where it was before. This time, teachers will be more disillusioned and disappointed than ever before.

Quadrant 2: High participation, low skillfulness

In a Quadrant 2 school, those in formal leadership positions may operate much of the time in a laissez-faire and unpredictable fashion (with intermittent periods of autocratic rule). Information, like programs and relationships, is fragmented, lacking any coherent pattern. For instance, because the school has no agreed-upon grading policies, some teachers are failing 70 percent of their students, often for absences or unfinished homework, while other teachers may not penalize for these transgressions. And because there is no schoolwide focus on teaching and learning, poor teaching sometimes goes unnoticed. There is a strong ethos of rugged individualism, with a few skilled entrepreneurs leading pockets of innovation and many other participants "doing their own thing." Roles and responsibilities are unclear. Although overall student achievement is static, disaggregated data show that a few students (primarily girls in the lower grades and boys in the higher grades, and those of higher socioeconomic status) are doing very well whereas others are doing poorly.

Quadrant 3: High skillfulness, low participation

A Quadrant 3 school may be making progress toward reforms. They have selected a small leadership team whose members, along with the principal, are gaining some powerful leadership skills. They have learned to use available data to make school decisions. However, only a few key teacher activists have become involved. Pockets of active resistance are strong and increasingly vocal. Those staff who find themselves in the lonely middle lack the skills to negotiate their ideas and work through stages of conflict with reluctant staff. Roles and responsibilities are unclear for those who are not among the designated leaders. There are pockets of strong innovation and excellent classrooms, but focus on student learning is not a schoolwide norm. Although student achievement is showing slight gains, the long-term pattern is similar to that found in Quadrant 2.

Belvedere Middle School, referred to in Chapter 1 and described more completely in Chapter 4, is a Quadrant 3 School. It has pockets of strong innovations, some skilled leaders, and strong resistance as well. Resistors have used the principal's leaving as an opportunity to block further progress and to throw into question the entire process of reform.

Quadrant 4: High skillfulness, high participation

A school with high leadership capacity has a principal capable of *collaboration* and inclusive leading. More than half of the staff have gained the leadership skills necessary to affect the norms, roles, and responsibilities of the school. *The schoolwide focus is on both student and adult learning.* Schoolwide inquiry generates and discovers information that informs practice and decisions. *Decision making is shared.* Information loops follow a spiraling process that keeps all informed and provides for reflective interpretation and construction of shared meaning (for examples, read the story of Capricorn High School in Chapter 5). Roles and responsibilities overlap, with each person taking personal and *collective responsibility* for the work of leadership. Staff describe themselves as being part of a professional community. *Student achievement is high.* Even disaggregated data show relatively little difference among socioeconomic or gender groups.

These four quadrants provide four scenarios of leadership capacity in schools. Of course, numerous other possible scenarios would blend many of these features in different combinations. For our purposes, I will use the indicators described here and offer assessment tools, stories, and strategies for your consideration. For instance, the Appendixes include staff and school assessment tools for estimating the level of leadership capacity in your school.

Critical Features of High Leadership Capacity

The work undertaken by Quadrant 4 schools is difficult. It needs to be informed and guided by skilled professionals who hold a firm vision of what it means to develop a school with high leadership capacity. The rich work now available on school reform can be distilled down to the elements in the matrix and the following five critical features of a successful school:

• Broad-based, skillful participation in the work of leadership

• Inquiry-based use of information to inform shared decisions and practice

- Roles and responsibilities that reflect broad involvement and collaboration
    - Reflective practice/innovation as the norm
    - High student achievement

The following sections describe each critical feature and the leadership dispositions, knowledge, and skills essential to the development of such a school. As noted earlier, Chapters 3 through 5 include specific stories of schools at each level of leadership capacity, the actions taken by their staffs, critical questions confronting each school, and suggested interventions and strategies. The matrix (Figure 2.1) and these five features are the backdrop for analyzing the school narratives.

Broad-based, skillful participation in the work of leadership

This feature is the essence of leadership capacity and requires attention to two areas: (1) structures and processes for participation and (2) opportunities to become skillful participants. (These correspond to the two axes on the Leadership Capacity Matrix—Participation and Skillfulness, respectively.)

A school needs several kinds of working groups. First, it needs governance groups that are representative of the school's many constituents: teachers, administrators, students, parents, community members, and, if possible, district office personnel and university faculty. Governance groups are charged with the authority to facilitate the decision-making processes in the school, engaging all faculty in those processes. Through mutual agreement, they will make some decisions directly; they will take others to the whole faculty. Governance groups, however, are just the beginning. Almost as important are the multiple groups needed for getting the work of the school done. These might include collaborative action research groups (ad hoc groups that all faculty serve on at least once) and grade-level and interdisciplinary teams. As stated in Chapter 1, collaborative work is directly linked to school improvement and to children's and adults' learning. Yet the work must be spread out and shared, so that staff are not overwhelmed with tasks. It is important to note that the work involves two kinds of changes or shifts: (1) taking on different roles and tasks, and (2) working differently; that is, communicating differently in individual and group conversations (asking questions, listening, giving feedback).

Opportunities for collaboration are not enough in and of themselves. Shared work that is not skillfully done can be nonproductive because it focuses, for example, on war stories, complaints, and tales of atypical students. The leadership skills needed for collaborative work involve the ability to develop a shared sense of purpose with colleagues, facilitate group processes, communicate well, understand transition and change and their effects on people, mediate conflict, and hold a keen understanding of adult learning from a constructivist perspective. Such a perspective enables us to create mutual trust, hear each other, pose questions and look for answers together, and make sense of our common work. Individuals can learn these perspectives and skills through observation and guided practice, coaching, skill-focused dialogue (talking through strategies and approaches), and training.

Inquiry-based use of information to inform shared decisions and practice

Renewal processes include reflection, dialogue, question posing, inquiry (including use of data), construction of new meaning and knowledge, and action. Faculty meetings that use these processes can be highly stimulating. For example, an agenda might call for the staff to reflect upon past successes and beliefs about teaching the Constitution. Questions are posed: "Are the students experiencing this the way we think they are? What do they think about the Constitution by the end of their junior year?" A few focus groups—and an examination of student projects—can provide some interesting answers from students that are shared with the rest of the faculty at the next meeting. The dialogue focuses on making sense of student responses in reference to staff experiences and beliefs. Working together, the staff might suggest alterations in how and where the Constitution is taught. This can be a natural and comfortable process. Even if all teachers are not teaching the Constitution, to the extent that others join in the inquiry and dialogue, this allows for a "tuning" process (McDonald, 1996) that is priceless for practice. By "tuning," McDonald means the improvement of the quality of the craft of teaching through hearing and considering feedback from multiple sources, both inside and outside the school.

Inquiry requires time—and it also requires rethinking how we use the time that we have, such as faculty meetings. Schools need to develop plans and schedules that create common time for dialogue and reflection. Often it is important to engage in proactive advocacy with the community, district, and political groups concerning the essential nature of professional time.

Even in the best of schools, polarization arises between those who are actively involved in change efforts and those who are holding back. A typical missing piece in reform efforts is a comprehensive information system that involves everyone at their varied stages of thinking and talking about the issues at hand. A communication system needs to keep all informed and involved through what are known as feedback loops. Information needs to accumulate and be reinterpreted as it moves through the school. For instance, if a school is considering block scheduling, staff members need to engage in numerous conversations to surface early concerns and ideas, interpret those concerns, and design strategies to work through problems. This could involve four or five rounds of small-scale conversations as concerns are heard and addressed. It cannot be done solely in writing or in whole faculty meeting pronouncements. It is essential that small, personal conversations take place about things that are happening in the school, how people are thinking and feeling about these developments, what ideas are occurring to them, and what meanings are emerging.

I have found that a useful strategy is to have a group such as a leadership team divide up the faculty among team members. For instance, each team member might take responsibility for six to eight faculty members with whom she or he regularly talks. Or a span of time—perhaps a week—can be set for a regular round of small conversations with others who have rooms nearby, who are in the same department or grade, who serve on similar teams, or who are chosen randomly. These small interactions can test the waters on ideas that are emerging in the team and invite new thoughts from faculty members. This fluid process weaves together the thinking and engagement of a staff in ways that diminish the likelihood of polarization.

Participation in shared governance groups is an important calling for a school leader. Each person should plan on doing this often during the course of a career. It is in such a setting that individuals can finely hone their leadership skills. Performed on a regular basis, the reciprocal learning processes can become familiar practice. Keep in mind that information will come to these groups in ways that are both formal (data and evidence) and informal (feedback loop conversations).

Roles and responsibilities that reflect broad involvement and collaboration

Growth in individual capacity brings about a change in self-perception and roles. As roles change, new behaviors emerge: staff members can speak before an adult group or analyze data, be persuasive with parents or district personnel, and ask critical questions. Teachers, particularly, no longer see themselves as responsible only for their classroom, but for the school as well. Old responses no longer work. A strong indicator of this shift is the questions that people ask in faculty rooms and meetings, and the items they suggest for agendas.

Consider the difference in the following items that individuals suggested for discussion over two years in an elementary school:

Year One
- Hours for individual aides
- Materials budget for each classroom
- Playground duty schedule
- Social committee report

Year Two
- Program review process
- K–6 reading program: How well are our students reading?
- Community participation in the school
- Professional development program

The scope of items changed in this school as teachers began to perceive their roles differently and to assume responsibility in a broader arena of work. These changes in perception took place as teachers were asked to reflect, to inquire, to construct meanings, and to rethink old actions (reciprocal learning processes). The year-one issues remained important, but the staff recognized the year-two issues as broader and more important in the long run.

The goal of shifting roles is to enable each participant to take responsibility for the classroom, the school, the community, and the profession. When faculty observe colleagues assuming responsibility outside of traditional roles, it is helpful to give feedback regarding that change. Such feedback might involve praising the idea, asking the next question ("and then what would happen if we . . . ?"), or asking how you can become involved in investigating this issue.

As roles change, relationships change. People see each other in a new light. They recognize new skills and resources in people they've known for years. As the opportunities for new ways of being together emerge, relationships can cut across former boundaries that had been established. For instance, 1st grade teachers find new reasons for talking with 4th grade teachers; English teachers find something in common with math teachers. As more of who we are becomes exposed, we find more in common with others.

Assuming responsibility for the agreements that the school community has made represents an important role shift. Agreements usually require that everyone's role change, and this can be done only with the full involvement of everyone affected. Otherwise the principal is cast as the "implementor," the person who must force the change on the school through edict, evaluation, supervision, or monitoring. Decisions need to be accompanied by explicit agreements about responsibilities for each aspect of the new or modified program.

Reflective practice/innovation as the norm

The cycle of inquiry described above has an essential reflective phase. Many forms of reflection must become an integral part of the school: reflection on beliefs, assumptions, and past practice (the first step in constructivism); reflection in action, in practice; collective reflection during dialogue and in coaching relationships. To make such habits of mind the norm, time must be available for reflection, a "language of reflection" must be part of the talk of the school (deliberate use of phrases like "I've been thinking about, pondering . . . ," "When I reflect upon . . . ," "I need to reflect about that"); reflection must be demonstrated and honored—but never used as an obstacle; rather it must be seen as the prelude before movement to action.

Reflection leads to the opportunity to "run with" an idea, to see it through. If the principal customarily blocks ideas, if discretionary resources are lacking, if there are restrictive policies or district unwillingness, the ideas are not likely to blossom on a regular basis. If a school community feels that an idea warrants a trial, many doors need to open to enable the inventors (entrepreneurs) to transform the idea into reality. Innovators should be encouraged to involve other colleagues, to establish responsible criteria for success, and to create a realistic time line for monitoring and evaluation.

High student achievement

The central focus of any school must be teaching and learning. Learning needs to be viewed as "authentic"—that is, based on real tasks that have a relationship to work and life in society or in the family. Curriculum, instruction, and assessment that are authentic involve performances and products that transfer into the actual world of citizenship as well as future scholarship. A comprehensive view of authentic relationships with children requires that teaching roles expand to include teacher as facilitator, mentor, coach, and advisor.

Information about student achievement gathered through performances and products is the most precious kind of information for inquiry and general improvement. This information needs to cycle back to students and parents as well—those who can help interpret the meaning of the information and help to refine instructional processes. Parents make fine pedagogical partners, for they have deep knowledge about how their children learn.

Student learning is the *content* of leadership. It is what we talk about, struggle with, decide about, plan for. Unless the reciprocal learning processes of leadership include student learning, we will have only process for the sake of process.

In this book, student achievement is broadly conceived and has several components:

• Academic achievement in work that is authentically performed and assessed whenever possible
• Positive involvement (good attendance, few suspensions, low dropout rate, high graduation rate, parent and student satisfaction)
• Resiliency behaviors (self-direction, problem solving, social competence, having a sense of purpose and future)

• Equitable gains across socioeconomic groups; improvement regardless of gender, race, or ethnicity

• Narrowed gaps between socioeconomic groups

• Sustained improvement over time, with improvement increasing and gaps narrowing the longer that students are exposed to school improvement factors

The Role of the Principal

Teachers must take the major responsibility for building leadership capacity in schools and ultimately for the work of school improvement. Teachers represent the largest and most stable group of adults in the school, and the most politically powerful (Lambert, Kent, Richert, Collay, & Dietz, 1997). However, the role of the principal is more important than ever. Sound contradictory?

Why is the role of the principal more important than ever? Because the work is much more complex than we thought it was; it demands a more sophisticated set of skills and understandings than ever before. It is more difficult to build leadership capacity among colleagues than to tell colleagues what to do. It is more difficult to be full partners with other adults engaged in hard work than to evaluate and supervise subordinates.

This hard work requires that principals and teachers alike serve as reflective, inquiring practitioners who can sustain real dialogue and can seek outside feedback to assist with self-analysis. These learning processes require finely honed skills in communication, group process facilitation, inquiry, conflict mediation, and dialogue. Further, these skills are generally not the focus of many professional preparation programs and must be refined on the job.

Principals' leadership is crucial because they are uniquely situated to exercise some special skills of initiation, support, and visioning. Among the more important tasks for the principal is to establish collegial relationships in an environment that may previously have fostered dependency relationships. For instance, teachers may have been accustomed to asking permission, waiting to discover clues of right behavior from the principal, expecting the principal to clarify goals and programs, receiving praise and criticism, being uninformed about the overall direction of the school. The principal may have derived much of her informal authority from teachers' expectations that she would behave in a benevolently authoritarian way. Breaking through this "codependency" arrangement requires staff to develop adult-to-adult relationships with each other. Here are a few examples of successful strategies for breaking codependent relationships:

- When a staff member asks the principal's permission for something he wants to do, she can redirect the question by asking, "What do you recommend?"
- When a staff group remains silent, waiting for "the answer" from the principal, the principal can say, "I've thought about this issue in three ways. . . . Help me analyze and critique these ideas," or "I don't know the answers. . . . Let's think it through together."
- When the staff have expectations about the role of the principal and refuse to take on responsibilities "because that is the principal's job," the principal can ask the staff to explicitly negotiate in a faculty meeting everyone's roles and responsibilities. During this discussion, the principal can clarify her perceptions and consider and discuss other expectations.
- When a teachers union objects to changing role expectations, those involved shouldn't accept the objection at face value; they should insist on a thorough discussion of the issue and opportunities for a negotiated reconsideration.

The first column of the Rubric of Emerging Teacher Leadership (Appendix C) describes many kinds of codependent and dependent behaviors.

Much of the vital work on student achievement described in this book comes from the studies of Newmann and Wehlage (1995, 1996). They did not ignore the role of the principal. They found that principals in successful restructuring schools demonstrate some consistent habits of leadership that are compelling in their clarity. Formal leaders in restructuring schools "gave central attention to building a schoolwide collective focus on student learning of high intellectual quality" (p. 291). By keeping issues of teaching and learning at the center of the dialogue, these leaders built organizational capacity in their schools. They consistently expressed the norms and values that defined the school's vision, initiated conversations, and provoked staff to think about that vision. They created time for reflective inquiry and staff development and shared power by being at the center of the school's organizational pattern. In a critically important role, they were conflict managers and politicians in the best sense, often seeking waivers, resources, and policies to support the restructuring work.

If such principals are teaching others in the school to understand what they are doing and to be able to behave in similar ways, we can say that these principals are the teachers of teachers when it comes to building leadership capacity. On the other hand, if key teachers want to move the school and it is the principal who is reluctant, teachers must educate the principal, making suggestions, posing questions, volunteering to take responsibility for certain tasks, and giving feedback.

Principals can use authority to reinforce and maintain dependent relationships or to establish and maintain processes that improve the leadership capacity of the school. To accomplish the latter, a principal can do the following:

• Develop a shared vision based on school community values by involving staff and community in a process that allows them to reflect upon their own cherished values, listen to those held by others, and make sense through dialogue of how to bring personal and community values together into a shared vision statement.

• Organize, focus, and maintain momentum in the learning dialogue by convening the group on a regular basis.

• Interpret and protect school community values, assuring both focus and congruence with teaching and learning approaches.

• Work with all participants to implement school community decisions.

These uses of authority will actually redistribute authority and power in a school so that a culture of peers—a professional community—can grow. The following strategies can help principals be highly effective in creating a culture of peers and building leadership capacity within the school:

• Posing questions that hold up assumptions and beliefs for reexamination
• Remaining silent, letting other voices surface
• Promoting dialogue and conversations
• Raising a range of possibilities but avoiding simplistic answers
• Keeping the value agenda on the table, reminding the group that what they have agreed on is important, focusing attention
• Providing space and time for people to struggle with tough issues
• Confronting data, subjecting one's own ideas to the challenge of evidence
• Turning a concern into a question
• Being wrong with grace, candor, and humility
• Being explicit and public about strategies, since the purpose is to model, demonstrate, and teach them to others

When a principal uses the authority of the position to convene and sustain the conversation, and demonstrates for a staff and school community the enabling behaviors listed above, the school is on a sure road toward building leadership capacity. The goal that focuses a principal's choice of behaviors is to enable more and more individuals to build their own informal authority and demonstrate leadership behaviors. The sum of these concerted efforts is broad-based, skillful participation in the work of leadership.

Arabesque Elementary School

Arabesque is a K–5 neighborhood school in a community dotted with turn-of-the century bungalows, 30-year-old apartment buildings, and a few small businesses. At one time, the community was fairly homogeneous, but the pattern has changed in the past two decades. Now the families come from diverse backgrounds—diverse in race and culture, as well as income and land of origin. There are no extremes in wealth, however; the families are mostly middle class and of Caucasian, Asian, or Hispanic descent. The school was built in 1954 in a compact, modular design that requires children and adults to go outside to move from one section of the school to another. A central courtyard with wooden tables is used for lunch on sunny days; otherwise tables are set up in a small gym that includes a stage on one side. The windows are high, and the old wine-colored velvet stage curtain has seen better days. In the playground, two giant oaks distinguish themselves, having long provided haven for children at play. Some of the residents of the nearby bungalows played there as children.

Many of the teachers are old-timers as well. A few began their careers in this school and plan to retire from here. The teachers have not grown much and are fixed in teaching patterns 20 or more years old. Their enthusiasm peaked many years ago; and without the stimulus of new challenges, their interests turned elsewhere. These interests are most often the subject of faculty conversations: the repertory season, the perils of small businesses, summer travel, gardening, and grandchildren. The social committee is a serious assignment, and birthdays and other holidays get important attention. Rarely do the teachers talk about teaching, and when they do, it is about a specific problem student or an unsupportive parent. If asked, they would say they are not unhappy as teachers at Arabesque.

These veteran teachers take their responsibility for the acculturation of new teachers very seriously as well. They tell new teachers about the history of the school and community and the changes that have led to lower achievement. They are wistful about the days when they could "expect more and get more." They are specific about the roles of the teachers, the principal, the school secretary, and the custodian. Teachers should focus on the classroom, maintaining the order and discipline essential to teaching. The tried and true methods of teaching are sound—don't throw them out for the next trendy idea to come along. Teachers are in for the long haul (a concept that administrators don't really understand). If you changed practice every time a new idea came along, it would be crazy-making! Never offend or seriously challenge those in charge of the school: the principal, the school secretary, and the custodian. These individuals try to keep the school on an even keel—don't expect more. If you are having a problem in the classroom, talk to one of your colleagues, but don't make a big deal of it. Expect certain requirements: once-a-month faculty meetings for announcements and event planning, issuing grades at the end of the quarter, calling parents back if they have a complaint, attendance at an occasional district staff development day. Evaluation? The principal will drop by for a few minutes, fill out the district checklist, and put it in your box. The district? They revise policy, ask for occasional reports, keep the board satisfied, and issue the paychecks. And, oh yes, a couple of years ago the principal instructed the teachers to move to "multigraded classrooms with interdisciplinary curriculum." But they didn't move far, and this directive hasn't fundamentally changed how they do things.

From 1973 to 1994, George Simpson was principal at Arabesque. He was loved by almost everyone. His style might be characterized as that of a "benevolent dictator." He cared about people, told stories with the best of them, and never embarrassed anyone by suggesting that they weren't doing a good job. George had the biggest retirement party ever seen in this community.

When George Simpson retired, the superintendent and several members of the board wanted some new ideas at Arabesque. Test scores had been slowly falling, real estate agents were not especially complimentary when the superintendent met up with them at Rotary meetings, and parents were beginning to question how things were being done. After careful advertising, paper screening, and interviewing, the superintendent decided to hire Sam Johnson. Although Sam was a little green, he was able to describe some new and exciting ideas for Arabesque. He was enthusiastic, he dressed well, and he came with glowing recommendations. Sam seemed to be the right person for the job.

That was three years ago. This week, Sam has been on the phone more than usual. Parents have been objecting to the new multigraded, teaming approaches, calling them disjointed, redundant, and poorly articulated. These were parents who couldn't be ignored or easily put off, Sam realized. The president of the PTA and a few of her friends had their fingers on the pulse of the community. They were probably reading the situation fairly correctly. The innovations were not going well. When the multigraded classrooms were implemented 18 months ago, Sam had hoped that the bugs would be worked out by now.

But deep down, Sam knew that he was kidding himself. The teachers had shied away from two practices that the literature said were essential to such change: collaborative planning and peer coaching. Peer coaching in particular was a concept that seemed far from their minds and traditions! What had gone wrong? Certainly he had approached these reforms carefully.

Three years ago—in his first faculty meeting at this school—he introduced his interests and intentions to move toward multi-graded classrooms with an interdisciplinary curriculum. By the winter break he had laid out the plans, the outcomes, and even the hoped-for effects on student achievement. The superintendent had attended that faculty meeting and told Sam that he'd done a "great job." During that first year, Sam had sent teachers to visit other schools and to attend workshops. He had even hired a couple of new teachers who had some knowledge of the innovations he was seeking to implement. No one had come to him with serious objections. He had assumed assent when there were few questions in the faculty meetings.

He realized that the agenda was pretty top-down, an approach that he rationalized in two ways. Wasn't it more honest to be direct with a vision and an agenda than to act as though it was okay to continue as things were? And his early attempts to implement some shared decision making had run into the only vocal opposition he'd experienced so far. A delegation of veteran teachers had come to him and said that principals were expected to make decisions at Arabesque. Further, the teachers would oppose any practice that would expect teachers to "do an administrator's work." Had he been wrong to interpret this session as granting him carte blanche? Frankly, Sam was relieved. He didn't have the time to implement all the innovations that he knew about, and he certainly didn't want to dilute the reforms. Shared decision making could come later.

One thing was crystal clear to Sam: in this district, principals were held accountable for the success or failure of schools. His fate as an administrator rested on the success of these innovations. "What should I do now?" he asked himself.

Arabesque and the Leadership Capacity Matrix

Arabesque had settled into Quadrant 1 of the Leadership Capacity Matrix (Figure 2.1 in Chapter 2), signifying low levels of participation and skillfulness in the work of leadership. Principals had assumed an autocratic, albeit benevolent, role. Relationships were primarily paternal in nature with rigidly defined roles, one-way communication, and codependent, compliant behaviors on the part of the teachers. Traditional practices stood fast against innovation and change. Memories of the good old days took the place of meaningful reflection. Student academic achievement was poor, and irregular attendance and playground conflict were persistent problems. Poor student performance was blamed on unsupportive families and changing demographics. The extensive work to be done at Arabesque needed to focus and move the school toward the critical features of Quadrant 4 of the Leadership Capacity Matrix.

Arabesque and the Critical Features of High Leadership Capacity

Broad-based, skillful participation in the work of leadership

Arabesque teachers have historically not been involved in the work of leadership. They have not taken responsibility for the growth and development of their colleagues, themselves, or even their students. They have used their influence to maintain the status quo, even to the point of acculturating new teachers into those norms. (Because this influence requires certain skills, the discussion below will propose some approaches for transforming *reactive* influence into *positive* influence.) Principals have been hired to meet the limited expectations held by the staff. And the principals have found comfort in autocratic behaviors. Principals who did not fit the mold were soon advised about proper administrative roles.

Inquiry-based use of information to inform shared decisions and practice

Staff at Arabesque have a firm sense of what they believe is happening to their students and their school. These perceptions are the direct outgrowth of ancient personal schemas uncluttered by inquiry or evidence. They point to the changing demographics, student and family profiles dictating the inevitability of poorer performance. Teachers are not systematically involved in high-priority decisions about teaching and learning, but they do use information to plan events (how many parents came to open house last year?), and they use test scores as the basis for selecting instructional materials.

Roles and responsibilities that reflect broad involvement and collaboration

Roles and responsibilities have remained traditional at Arabesque. Staff focus on the classroom, social interactions with other staff, and maintenance of a reactive posture toward school and district requirements. Collaboration to improve teaching and learning is rare. When resistance by the staff proves insufficient, a teachers union representative from the high school may file a grievance on their behalf. Principals are administrators who keep the school running (fix the furnace), manage classified personnel, and ward off negative reactions from parents and the district office through comforting but shallow rhetoric that provides protective coloring. This "protective" role is at the heart of the school's paternalism. Parents are to keep hands off unless their activities raise money for the school. Students are "receivers" of knowledge in the classic sense; direct teaching is the norm.

Reflective practice/innovation as the norm

Arabesque staff see themselves as reflective, a word they liken to nostalgic "remembering." Although remembering the history of the school is an important element in moving forward, these memories at Arabesque serve only to reinforce the status quo and the pining for the good old days. Reflection done in the company of others for the purpose of rethinking practice does not occur at Arabesque. Nor does innovation, unless imposed from above. Even imposed innovation, because it is not supported and not reinforced by collaborative work, soon becomes indistinguishable from regular practice.

High student achievement

Over the years, Arabesque has experienced small "bumps" in student achievement scores: short-term improvements based on some technical changes. However, it is safe to say that student learning has not improved. In fact, as the changing demographics have brought children from different cultures and learning styles to the school, the old ways have become progressively less successful. Teachers do not take responsibility for student learning but blame failures on external forces. Therefore, the rhetoric of blame has become louder, signaling an inevitable community crisis in the making. This impending crisis has caused the district, and now the new principal, to seek to bring about significant changes in classroom organization and teaching.

Strategies for Improving Low Leadership Capacity

Arabesque is an entrenched school. It is a vivid example of the systemic relationship among all the elements in a school, with those elements interacting to create an intractable situation. A paternalistic system; a staff colonized by a dominant, hierarchical district; principals and teachers who thrived on the system the way it was; an unquestioning community—all of these factors have colluded to create a poor school with low leadership capacity. The educators, students, and parents in this school are *no different from those found in many places*. They are captured by an environment that brings out certain behaviors that do not work in schools; for that matter, these behaviors do not work in any setting.

How do we get a handle on this situation? What are the critical points of intervention that will loosen the intractable parts and start the system breathing again?

The major challenge at Arabesque is to engage and focus the attention of faculty on their practice and connect their performance with student learning: building the responsibility connection. This is certainly not the only challenge confronting the school, but it is the most fundamental and difficult.

Altering the beliefs and the culture at a school like Arabesque requires a skillful change agent, usually the principal. This person can also be an outside school coach or consultant if that person is respected by the school community. In either case, the person must have access to formal authority that can be used in the ways described in Chapter 2.

After three years, Sam was transferred to another school, so the changes at Arabesque began with a new principal—a person more suitable for this context. Although Sam had many strengths, he misjudged the situation when he perceived his first level of work at Arabesque as innovation in teaching and learning; in fact, his first level of work needed to be attention to the dysfunctional adult culture, accompanied by some quick classroom successes.

Initially, in a situation like that at Arabesque, it is essential to capture the attention and respect of the veteran faculty. The following suggestions are possible approaches—they are not "right answers" or one "right way."

The new principal, Sarah Green, undertook a number of strategies and tactics. To get to know the faculty, she asked each person to come in before school started to get acquainted (all but one accepted the invitation). During this personal "interview" she asked teachers about family and aspirations, how they felt about the school, what was of highest value to them, what they would like to see improved. She listened respectfully without expectations or declarations.

She made some quick, short-term changes before school started (replacing the copy machine, opening the supply closet, streamlining the attendance form, painting the faculty room, buying round tables for the library). She credited these changes to the faculty, and rightly so, for they had suggested them. As school began, she would focus on short-term, visible changes that made people feel they had been listened to.

Fall faculty meetings included some of the leadership learning processes described in Chapter 1. Sarah particularly sought to hold discussions that would surface the experiences, histories, perceptions, and beliefs of faculty. These discussions led to the development of a "histomap" in October. On a large sheet of butcher paper, faculty traced their memories of the past 20 years, including changes in principals, district and state mandates, personal tragedies, community crises. The principal ended the meeting with a low-key, "Well, where do we go from here?"

At the next meeting, she began by summarizing the map exercise and the concerns she had heard from faculty during the personal interviews. She noted the quick changes that had been made. "Now, what is our next level of concern . . . what are we still troubled by?" She asked faculty to talk with each other at the table and decide on a couple of key ideas. The top issues were discipline and homework. She was not surprised, for she knew that these two topics inevitably rise to the top when substantial cultural change is initiated. "If these are our main concerns, I feel very strongly that we need to find out what the current situation is. We have important evidence in your observations and experiences. We also need to look at the referral and achievement data—and we need to know why children are not doing their homework." Looks of consternation and puzzlement appeared on a few faces, but several people volunteered for two ad hoc groups (Discipline and Homework).

During the fall and early winter, the principal gave top attention to communication and visibility. She was in the halls, in the faculty room, and in and out of classrooms giving positive feedback. Occasionally, when she felt the teacher was receptive, she would offer a quick idea that she had used or seen used—an idea that the teacher could quickly and confidently implement, such as three ways to get class convened. She relied heavily on her cognitive coaching training and particularly gave attention to some powerful questions that she had used to shift responsibility inward. These questions included the following:

- "Would you tell me about what the students are doing?"
- "This is interesting; tell me what you are doing here."
- "What went on in your head when the students responded in that way?"
- "What do you look for in students' reactions that tells you if students understand your directions?"
- "How will you decide what to do next?"
- "What do you think might have caused that?"
- "As you envision the next lesson, what do you see yourself doing?"

Sarah gave particular attention to supporting and coaching new teachers who were hungry for feedback and ideas to improve their practice. Her coaching skills, plus a few "minilessons" designed to address trouble spots, provided welcome interchanges. She was careful not to intervene in the relationships that new teachers had with veteran teachers. However, new teachers became more bold in asking veteran teachers questions about teaching and learning.

She attended faculty ad hoc meetings and, when an opportunity arose, she demonstrated facilitation skills. At the large faculty gatherings, she modeled how to manage productive meetings, giving her rationale for meeting designs. For instance, "Let's take a careful look at the agenda. We'll use 10 minutes to brainstorm our ideas, then take turns advocating for our preferences. Can we agree to have the revised agenda completed by 9:30?"

It seemed too early to this principal to organize a sophisticated leadership team, so she asked the faculty to nominate teachers whom they trusted to represent them on an advisory council. This group began to operate in the second semester of her first year. Its function was to serve as a clearinghouse for data and evidence about the school, to develop a process map (the sequence of events) for the work at hand, to plan faculty meetings, to develop a communication system, and to converse about effective change processes.

It was critical that an effective communication system be put into place (a forerunner of feedback loops). A weekly letter to staff pulled together everything happening in the school, including the procedures of the advisory council and the key decisions of the school board. A small statement appeared at the bottom of the letter: "There are no secrets." Advisory council and ad hoc committee members were asked to continually talk with their colleagues about what they were doing. At parent meetings, the principal openly discussed the school's struggles and decisions in process, and sought ideas and feedback. She placed the budget print-out from the district on the faculty room table with an invitation to ask questions and make suggestions.

The principal held regular meetings with classified staff, particularly the secretary and the custodian. The classified staff had ruled the roost, often intimidating new teachers. In these meetings—and in between—a major point was consistently made: we are here for the kids, the parents, the teachers. We are here to help each one of them succeed. If teachers want to move their chairs, we encourage it. If teachers need access to phones and supplies, we encourage it. When parents walk in the door, we look up, smile, and help them immediately.

By January, relationships were beginning to form in new ways, and the staff had made some decisions about discipline and homework (by the beginning of the third year, they had modified these decisions to make them more consistent with the vision of the school). In a half-day workshop, faculty and classified staff (with a few parents) convened to consider the school's vision and goals. The staff summarized what they had learned in the fall about their history, values, and interests. They examined evidence of student achievement, behavior problems, and faculty perceptions of problem areas. They developed a scenario about what they would like their school to be like for children (brainstorming key elements and combining them into a short description) and identified five goals to work on for the balance of the year. They agreed to review these decisions at the opening of school the following year.

Frequent conversations with the superintendent led to a policy proposal to the school board requesting early release on Wednesdays. (Although this is not a unique strategy, it was new for this district.) The board approved the proposal. The shortened days began in March and gave the teachers time to do the necessary planning. (Summer workshops, an occasional whole day, paid "after work" time, or other techniques would serve the same purpose—although not quite as well as regular and consistent time.)

The principal knew that one of her most challenging undertakings would be breaking the codependent relationship between the principal and the staff. When the staff asked for permission or came to her for the "right" answer, she redirected the conversation with questions that sought the staff members' insights, opinions, advice. When staff proclaimed "this is not my responsibility," she refused to take the issue on herself but insisted on working it through with the staff. She was careful not to signal limited expectations for the staff and did not accept the circumscribed role that had historically been the principal's "cage." She also casually announced that she expected to be at Arabesque for the "long haul"—to see things through.

During the process of breaking codependencies, there is a danger that old-timers will interpret these actions as weakness or inability to make a decision. To counteract such charges, it is important to model resolute, firm, and decisive behaviors in areas in which principals appropriately exercise authority, such as convening the staff to discuss student data or to work on designing professional development opportunities.

Some observers might say that Sarah didn't accomplish much that first year. Arabesque did not witness major changes in student achievement, although there were fewer discipline referrals and fewer altercations on the playground. However, anger and hurt were diminished and diffused by respectful listening and involvement. Communication was open for the first time, including in the areas of school budget and district expectations. The leadership structure was changing as staff became involved with committees, the advisory council, and meaningful conversations. The staff were consistently directing attention toward the teaching and learning agenda. The culture was beginning to change significantly.

The processes that made a difference at Arabesque can be highly effective in middle schools and high schools as well, as we will see in Chapters 4 and 5.

BELVEDERE MIDDLE SCHOOL

THIS BOOK BEGAN WITH A DILEMMA POSED BY BELVEDERE MIDDLE School. This chapter tells Belvedere's story in more detail. The school's journey, as well as the dilemma, is a common one. Belvedere is a school caught in midstream, familiar territory for many schools. The transitional issues that faced Belvedere when the principal left are critical to our understanding of school change. Equally critical is the role played by the school district in hiring a new principal and reframing its expectations for the school.

In 1993, the school board had officially changed Belvedere Junior High to Belvedere Middle School. The decision was primarily motivated by the burgeoning population in the elementary schools, which forced a move to open up more K–5 classrooms. The board made the decision quickly in response to an opportunity made available by the state to reduce class size in 1st through 3rd grade to a maximum of 20 children. Little thought or planning went into the question "What does it mean to be a middle school?" The assistant superintendent had eloquently described the middle school possibilities at the decisive board meeting: a transitional 6th grade year, improved guidance, more choices/electives, integrated curriculum, and better preparation for high school.

Those ideas remained dormant on the pages of the assistant superintendent's report during the 1993–94 school year. Belvedere was still a junior high in design and spirit. "Secondary" teachers organized into departments taught five of the six periods per day. Guidance was a function of counselors; extracurricular activities were restricted to intramurals and competition among schools. Discipline was a frequent topic at heated faculty meetings. Like so many junior highs, Belvedere was a "mini–high school."

Built in 1968, Belvedere's architectural design featured "pods" of classrooms clustered around a central library in a hexagon pattern. The design encouraged opportunities for physical closeness and potential integration, although teachers had created barriers of file cabinets to ensure greater privacy. The library—yet to boast a modicum of technological upgrading—was used when English teachers brought in their classes to complete research reports.

Community expectations, particularly in the areas of discipline and career choices, varied significantly (at least this was thought to be so). At one end of Belvedere's rectangular attendance area was the country club and the spacious homes that fronted on the green; at the other end was a closed naval base, part of which had been turned into low-cost housing. The two ends were separated by middle class homes, condominiums, and a few apartment buildings. The community was racially and culturally diverse, with a recent upswing in Asian American families of modest means. The majority of parents in this suburban community commuted to a large metropolitan center 30 miles away.

In the spring of 1994, the district superintendent left and the assistant superintendent became superintendent. She was determined to see Belvedere become a "real middle school." After an exhaustive search, the district hired Maria Sanchez, an experienced middle school principal. Clearly charged with the responsibility to "make Belvedere into a middle school," Maria began her work at Belvedere in the fall of 1994.

Maria brought a track record for successful restructuring. She had a high respect for teachers and faith in the aspirations of parents and children. As teachers worked in their rooms just before school opened and during the first few days of school, Maria visited each staff member. Other teachers and the secretary introduced her around. She asked those who had played a strong leadership role in the school to drop by before school started. "Fill me in," she said. "Tell me about Belvedere and what has happened here."

During the fall the faculty agreed to form a formal leadership team, nominated and selected by the faculty. They discussed the role of the team and member rotation. The team, made up of four key teachers, the attendance clerk, and the principal, agreed to meet on Tuesdays after school. In November, they attended team training at the county office, learning such skills as communication, facilitation, and conflict management.

The team planned a faculty retreat in January, to be held during two back-to-back staff development days. Although there was some dissension over an overnight trip with other faculty, strong district support encouraged almost full participation (2 faculty members out of a staff of 37 called in sick).

The January retreat was a historic event for Belvedere staff. They talked about what they believed and valued, outlined a rough vision statement, and decided to form small task forces to begin work on three top-priority items: (1) early adolescence and its meaning for middle school curriculum, (2) the organization of the 6th grade, and (3) parent participation. At this point, 15 of the 37 faculty were explicitly involved in one of the teams.

By spring the three task forces reported on what they had learned from their visits to other middle schools, their reading of research, and their surveys of parents and students. For the first time, opposition became apparent, particularly in reference to a new middle school curriculum. Although the discussion of early adolescent qualities and needs was engaging and satisfying, with broad-based agreement, somehow the agreement broke down when it came to translating those needs into curriculum and organization. The need for guidance and support was evident, but staff did not feel comfortable providing it; engaging students actively in their own learning—rather than lecturing them—proved difficult to plan. Some staff felt they were being asked to "start over" as teachers.

The staff tentatively agreed to an initial plan for improved parent participation, and they decided to table the other reports until fall. "Perhaps we're moving too fast," reflected Maria.

During the 1995–96 school year, Belvedere made steady progress as the leadership team kept the agenda focused. Six teachers volunteered to explore peer coaching. Students formed their own leadership team that met before school. A group of volunteer teachers agreed to staff a 6th grade core of integrated English and social studies for the spring semester. The school created a new master schedule to accommodate the changes.

Maria took on a "servant" role in relation to the leadership team and task forces. She gathered data and provided it to the teams. She also served as a clearinghouse for information and communication. A weekly letter updated staff on the progress being made by teacher leaders. The vice principal continued to concentrate largely on discipline, student activities, and his share of teacher evaluations, but he was a good partner and listener.

At times Maria realized that the "big picture" might reside only in her head, but things were going well. Pockets of innovation (pairs of peer coaches, some project-based learning, a community service expectation in social studies) were growing, and she could see improvements in many classrooms, particularly those using constructivist and cooperative learning strategies. Although it was too early to expect changes in standardized test scores, there were improvements in attendance, behavior, and grades (particularly among 6th graders).

At faculty meetings, faculty leaders led discussions on the progress they were making in each area of improvement. Maria knew that some faculty were holding out—occasionally grumbling about expectations to "lower standards in order to become friends to these kids," even though she and several teachers said more than once that higher standards were the goal. She continued to treat those individuals with respect and trusted that they would come to share her sense of urgency about middle school reform.

The superintendent was pleased with the progress at Belvedere. She could see the program improvements, and parents were becoming more positive in the comments they made at district meetings and public gatherings. There was no doubt that the community was beginning to have faith in the work being done at the new middle school. Belvedere teachers were invited to participate in district committees, workshops, and presentations. It was in such a setting that Jennifer Fielding, the teacher we met in Chapter 1, decided to transfer to Belvedere.

In the spring of 1997, Maria announced that she was resigning to accept an assistant superintendency is a nearby district. She was somewhat surprised by the faculty response. Those teacher leaders with whom she had worked most directly were happy for her but felt a sense of betrayal. "You're strong enough to continue this work," she argued. "We are over the major hurdles. You are skilled in leading the faculty. And the district has assured me that they will find a principal who will be a compatible partner and continue the agenda you've set for yourselves." Those who had most resisted the reforms became more vocal: "She couldn't stick it out. We knew some of these ideas were impractical. Just like a principal to get things started that she can't finish. Perhaps now we can get back to our real work."

The district did not hire a new principal until August, so plans for the beginning of the school year were not well thought out. He had little opportunity to talk with teacher leaders or anyone else on the staff. Fortunately, the master schedule had been built to retain the 6th grade core and the student leadership class, but the 7th grade interdisciplinary teams and the 8th grade electives had not been adequately staffed or planned during the intervening summer. Those who had participated in leading the restructuring efforts seemed disillusioned and angry in the fall of 1997. Those who had resisted felt vindicated.

Belvedere and the Leadership Capacity Matrix

Belvedere represents a blend of Quadrants 2 and 3 of the Leadership Capacity Matrix (see Figure 2.1 in Chapter 2). The principal was a thoughtful, focused educator whose behaviors revealed three shortcomings that arrested progress at the school: (1) she and a few teachers were the primary communicators, and she was the primary source of data; (2) she was unable to confront and mediate the growing opposition among some teachers; and (3) she left the school too early in the reform process. The shortcomings translated into limited use of data for decision making and a lack of coherence of both information and programs. Staff were increasingly polarized as the chasm developed between teacher-leaders and staff who perceived themselves to be on "the outside."

On the other hand, pockets of innovation had resulted in pockets of improvement in student performance. Classrooms using innovative approaches had fewer discipline referrals, whereas traditional classrooms had more. Overall, by the third year, student achievement on standardized measures showed a slight improvement.

As in the case of Arabesque Elementary School, the work at Belvedere needed to move the school toward the critical features of Quadrant 4 of the Leadership Capacity Matrix.

Belvedere and the Critical Features of High Leadership Capacity

Broad-based, skillful participation in the work of leadership

By the time Maria left in the spring of 1997, about 30 percent of the Belvedere staff were actively involved in some aspects of the reform. Another 20 percent (primarily new teachers) were sympathetic and cooperative. However, pockets of resistance were strong. The involved teachers had become skilled in planning sequences of events, designing and facilitating interactive meeting agendas, and reflecting upon and assessing their progress. These are significant skills. However, certain terrain had been occupied by only the principal or had not been explored at all. Foremost among these untouched skill areas were conflict management (surfacing, confronting, and working through conflict), communication, and inquiry. Maria had assumed the major responsibility for communication and for collecting and organizing evidence about the school. When respect and courtesy were insufficient to win over reluctant staff, she rode it out, hoping that things would change.

Inquiry-based use of information to inform shared decisions and practice

Although the leadership team at Belvedere used information and evidence to make decisions, they had not involved other members of the staff in the inquiry process itself. The principal had discovered and synthesized data and evidence. The staff understood data as numbers and did not accord equal importance to such rich qualitative data as observations, interviews, and focus groups. Teachers had yet to trust their own observations and interpretation of student work as important evidence.

The general communication system was composed of written information, a one-way approach that did not seek feedback, interactions, and new interpretations. Faculty meetings did provide for interaction and dialogue—critical features of a communication system—but this pattern did not continue between meetings.

The peer coaching teams were able to generate insights and strategies that improved practice in the pilot classrooms, but a system for sharing these improvements was not yet in place. When staff attempted to share the results of these collaborative efforts, resistant teachers became sarcastic or silent—either action served to intimidate the experimenting teachers.

Roles and responsibilities that reflect broad involvement and collaboration

There were some important role changes among participating teachers at Belvedere. These teachers were beginning to see themselves as facilitators of adult learning, change agents, reform planners. They were sensitive barometers within the changing culture. As decision makers and problem solvers, they had developed meeting agendas that were crisp yet allowed for consideration of evidence and dialogue. Their actions and instincts were collaborative and open.

As a group, teacher roles covered the full spectrum of professional role development. At one end of the spectrum, teachers were focusing exclusively on the classroom as lone practitioners, assuming a rather passive role in group gatherings. Many teachers were in transitional passages, beginning to work collaboratively to reflect upon practice and engaging in productive dialogue in organized meetings. At the professional end of the spectrum, teachers were taking responsibility for leading the reforms, implementing community decisions, mentoring new teachers, and reaching beyond the school to influence the district and the region. The problem was that this process needed at least one more year to include enough teachers to take root.

The role of the vice principal was narrowly defined. Because he focused primarily on student behavior and activities, he did not understand the whole picture of the restructuring effort; therefore, it was difficult for him to provide transitional leadership when the principal left. The principal had retained the major leadership role, including responsibility for inquiry and communication, and especially including communication with the district office.

Reflective practice/innovation as the norm

Despite strong pockets of reflective practice, such practice was not the norm. The 6th grade core and peer coaching teams were making time to talk about their work and learning from each other. Overall, public examination of practice was in its initial stages.

The staff and community as a whole had come to expect innovations in the "middle school" vein. They understood the needs of early adolescence and the intent to translate those needs into programmatic changes: advisement, integrated curriculum, block scheduling, electives, new roles for parents, and an array of student activities. In spite of the planned innovative path, the actual changes tended to come more from earlier commitments to a reform agenda and the current educational "trends" than from the practice of inquiry and problem finding and resolution within the school. Thus, for some staff, the plans felt top-down, not to mention too general to implement.

Other than at faculty meetings, there was no organized time for peer coaching, team development, and other reflective practices. The school and the district had not found acceptable ways to support the need for reflective time during the school day. An effort to carve out collaborative work time on Mondays by lengthening class times Tuesday through Friday had met with union opposition. The school needed more time and effort toward compromise to work this out.

High student achievement

Belvedere students were beginning to make small gains. Although standardized test scores showed little difference, behavior factors such as attendance, classroom discipline problems and referrals, and school ground conflicts were showing improvement. Students were more involved in goal setting and decision making, including creating plans for their own performance. In general, however, students and parents were still outside the information/feedback loop; that is, parents were informed but not involved in setting new performance goals.

The innovations had brought about more constructivist classrooms, particularly in the 6th grade core and the classrooms of teachers involved in peer coaching. Content remained important, but more of the learning was coming from student inquiry and experimentation. Faculty were talking about authentic assessment; a pilot portfolio was underway in English classes. The elementary feeder schools were bringing pressure on the school to move to more authentic assessment ("We'll be passing on our students' portfolios at the end of the year. What plans do you have to use them?"). But classroom improvements and student achievements were irregular, testimony to the spottiness of reform at Belvedere.

Strategies for Improving Moderate Leadership Capacity

It would be seductive for a new principal to bring a whole new agenda, his own innovations, to Belvedere. However, such an action would constitute a death knell for reform at this school in the foreseeable future.

Fortunately, at the urging of teacher leaders at Belvedere, the district used an excellent selection process to find a new principal. The search was not easy. It had to be reopened twice—accounting for the delay in bringing the new principal on board in time for spring or summer planning. Teachers, parents, and students played a major role in setting the selection criteria, paper screening, visiting candidates' schools, and formal and informal interviewing. Candidates were asked to develop a written product, interact as in a planning meeting, and observe a teaching episode and conduct a follow-up coaching session with the teacher.

By August, the selection committee had hired John Trevor as the new principal. John was an experienced middle school principal, but he knew that the challenge at Belvedere was unique. After meeting with teacher leaders and many others both within and outside the school, he assessed the challenge to be one of reclaiming and building on the reforms and commitments established in the first three years, breaking through the barriers inhibiting further progress and change, and assuring staff that he would be around to see it through. He would seek to define his role as colleague of the teacher leaders at the school, supporter of current reforms, learner, and facilitator. It would be important for him to work as a collaborative peer, not "reclaiming" any of the authority that had already been redistributed.

The teacher-leaders became John's coaches, and John was able to bring some new skills in change and conflict management, coaching, and communication to the team. To confront the challenges before them, John and the teacher-leaders undertook a number of approaches and strategies.

John used many of the same trust-building approaches as the previous principal. He personally reached out to staff, getting to know and listen to them without judgment. Yet, unlike the situation at Arabesque, the team knew that they could not wait until trust was established with John to make some major moves.

The leadership team asked faculty to conduct a process to select two new members. At an all-day Saturday planning session, the team reviewed their achievements, selected their priorities, and refocused their agenda.

John—and the team—sought to bridge the distance between the two administrations by "pacing and leading." This meant that in each of their interactions and in faculty meetings they would recall and recapture where they had been in order to build a pathway to "what happens next?" For instance, a team member might say, "We've made great strides at broad-based involvement here with our leadership team, ad hoc groups, coaching, and interdisciplinary teams. How will we get even more people involved?"

As a critical aspect of the pace-and-lead approach, team members often restated the school's vision as they talked. Team members sat down with staff to seek clarification of the meaning of the vision statement, particularly in reference to what they hoped for in student achievement. They would often ask, "How will we know when we are doing this? What will it look like?"

The leadership team and staff were unfamiliar with alternative communication processes. They agreed, however, that this was an area that needed attention. One-way communication had reinforced passivity. John framed the process of developing better communication by working with the leadership team to pose a few critical planning questions:

- How can we organize ourselves to hold personal conversations with each staff member about issues and decisions?
- What decision-making processes provide opportunities for the staff and broader community to interpret and discuss issues, thereby accumulating feedback for the key groups involved?
- What forms of written communication are efficient in assisting group understanding and feedback?
- How can the staff organize, both in meetings and outside of meetings, to maximize interactions about issues important to the school?
- How can we involve the community and the district in these communication processes?
- How can we ensure that our communication system includes opportunities for reflection, dialogue, and inquiry?

The team assessed the nature of the struggle that teachers were having with each other. Teacher-leaders noted that some resistant teachers had significant personal power. These resistors knew just what to say—and when—to quiet their colleagues. John began to model positive confrontation and to coach teacher-leaders in mediation and conflict management work.

In the limited ventures into the use of data to inform decisions and practice, staff had tended to define data as numbers. Although these data made important contributions to the work at Belvedere, this perception also limited the deeper understandings that can be discovered through qualitative research approaches. John suggested that they redefine data more broadly as "evidence," and he talked about the validity of student work products and performances, classroom observations, interviews, focus groups, and dialogue sessions.

By late fall, the leadership team was able to introduce structured reflective practices at faculty meetings. Team members introduced an abridged form of the "protocol,"[1] conversations about student work, and case studies written by teachers about action research as an approach to whole-school change, and they actively supported the expansion of peer coaching. Recognizing that the staff needed to assess what they were doing and discover some of their own innovations, the team redefined the inquiry process as a legitimate path to full faculty participation.

The leadership team and the other staff clearly defined and articulated what they meant by "district support." High on the list were two items: (1) the need for "prime time" for adult collaborative work and (2) decentralized resources. (For other aspects of this strategy, see Chapter 6.)

The school's leaders agreed to break the "norm of silence" (i.e., "I won't talk with you about anything you're uncomfortable with"). They knew that comprehensive implementation of the school's reforms required that everyone get on board. With a focused agenda, a clear priority for offering an excellent program for every student, and some new perspectives and skills, the staff set about to expand the school's programs into every classroom.

By the next summer, three teachers had asked for a transfer to another school. Other staff assumed responsibility for implementation of their agreed-upon innovations (advisement, performance-based assessment, peer coaching, parent participation).

---

[1]"Protocol" is a dialogue tool used by teams of teachers to reflect on their learning. Typically, one team talks about student work or school change efforts, and the other team asks clarifying questions and gives critical feedback.

Although these approaches and strategies took time and had to be undertaken in a sensible sequence, Belvedere did not lose much momentum in its reform efforts. Thanks to teacher leadership, a thoughtful district hiring process, and an experienced and reflective principal, Belvedere was able to consolidate its gains and move forward.

CAPRICORN HIGH SCHOOL

IMPROVING THE AMERICAN HIGH SCHOOL HAS BEEN A GOAL of educators for generations. Current trends in this quest include establishing and raising standards, increasing time in school, increasing academic requirements while decreasing the number of choices, school-to-work and school-to-career programs, schools of choice and privatization, and the principles of major reform initiatives such as the Coalition of Essential Schools, the Comer Project, and John Goodlad's National Network for Educational Renewal. Building leadership capacity is not just another option in this array of approaches. Building leadership capacity is essential if *any* of these approaches is going to be successful.

Building leadership capacity is fundamental to all reform initiatives; but I do have preferences among these initiatives. The principles of the Coalition of Essential Schools (e.g., small schools, adult-student ratio of 1 to 80, constructivist teaching, performance-based assessment) constitute one of the most promising approaches. However, the Coalition suffers from the problems attendant to any movement with predetermined principles and limited attention to how those changes occur.

Capricorn High School is not a perfect school. It is a school with high leadership capacity that is on its way to becoming an exemplary school. The challenge at the center of this story is the consideration and implementation of block scheduling. Three conversations reveal the issue of "time for learning" and its inherent dilemmas.

Capricorn is a diverse, urban high school in a Midwestern town. The main building of the school is a large brick structure built in the 1930s. The gym and shops are in separate buildings connected by sidewalks, grass, and occasionally mud. The 1,600 students represent a racial and ethnic mix: 42 percent African American, 36 percent Caucasian, 12 percent Southeast Asian, and small numbers of Hispanics and Native Americans. Most of the staff live immediately outside the urban boundary, and 37 percent have taught in the school for more than 20 years. Five years ago, the school had a traditional and familiar profile: heavy tracking; isolated departments; top-down management; curriculum based almost solely on textbooks; norm-referenced and teacher-made paper and pencil tests; and significant achievement gaps among ethnic groups.

Five years ago, Bill Johnson came to Capricorn as principal. Bill is an unassuming, thoughtful individual. He has a keen sense of systemic thinking and a willingness to examine all school systems and structures, including discipline, attendance monitoring, parent involvement, athletics, and the role of those in formal authority positions. He convened the faculty for dialogue on the school's critical issues, and although he immediately met with opposition, his persistence and candor eventually earned the respect of the staff and a readiness to engage in inquiry-based restructuring. The unrelenting frequency and penetrating vigor of staff dialogue about student achievement broke through decades of blame and displaced responsibility.

Two years into the process, the school joined the Coalition of Essential Schools, and several staff members became active in other change-oriented networks. Working collaboratively and learning new instructional skills along the way, the faculty has eliminated tracking; initiated performance-, product- and community-based learning; begun to use student exhibitions; and implemented a schoolwide collaborative action research approach to program development and evaluation. Student achievement has improved in complex ways, including some narrowing of performance gaps among ethnically and culturally diverse students.

The story of Capricorn is portrayed here in portions of three conversations: two at general faculty meetings and one among a smaller group of faculty members. The first conversation took place two days after a regional high school network meeting that had focused on block scheduling. The network meeting was one of the quarterly gatherings at which the 70 participating schools addressed issues of current interest.

Faculty conversation I: Beginning an inquiry process

Faculty meetings at Capricorn are held in the school library, a place that is the center of active learning throughout the day. The large, high-ceilinged room has small study rooms for groups of students and faculty, an up-to-date collection of books and journals, multimedia resources, computers hooked to the Internet for student and faculty research, and an artistically created environment of posters and student work. Community support, special grants, and ingenuity were responsible for such abundance at a time when everything else seemed subject to reexamination and possible cutting.

A history teacher, Joan, chaired and led this particular faculty meeting. She asked the team that attended the regional meeting on block scheduling to describe what they had learned. Teachers, administrators, counselors, parents, students, and classified staff all participated in the conversation.

The team, still enthusiastic from their recent experience, first described what they had learned were the strengths of block scheduling, including opportunities for curricular depth, more complex teaching strategies (such as labs and simulations), better relationships with students and among students, and responsibility for fewer students per day. On the reverse side, there were political issues to negotiate with both staff and community, certain subjects that seemed more in need of daily practice, the need to learn new instructional strategies and a more varied repertoire, and the perception that comprehensive high schools should teach many subjects each day.

"Since we began our reforms, we knew that block scheduling would soon be on the table. It was just a matter of time," confessed Julie. "I'm ready to take a closer look."

"Let's take a few of these issues and examine them," said Teresa. "What is really meant by 'less is more'? In a comprehensive high school charged with preparing students for the university and an increasingly complex life, can less really be more?"

"My take on that Coalition of Essential Schools slogan, Teresa, refers to both fewer major concepts and more depth in those concepts. This builds on what we know about constructivism and clustering big ideas so that students will make connections and learn them well. The superficiality of a 'thin and broad' curriculum has not served our students well. Yes, we have tried to address those problems by integrating some of the curriculum, teaching cross-curricular skills, and occasionally teaming, but we are still slaves to the seven-period day. If I had more time with each student. . . ."

"What you describe as slavery, John, I think of as a daily opportunity for repetition, reinforcement, practice, an opportunity to work with mathematics in a way that will develop mathematical thinking. Can I be assured that one of the daily three or four blocks of time will be devoted to math?"

"No, Carol, you can't, any more than I can expect one of those periods to be devoted to foreign language. And I have the same concerns."

"There's another issue that I would like to place on the table," declared Ashley, president of the student body. "When hundreds of kids pour into the halls at the same time—six times a day!—my locker gets rattled and so do I. We have too much to get done in five minutes. I watch kids jostle each other, racing to go to the locker, the bathroom, and talk with their friends. If we could reduce the number of passing periods, I would be all for it."

"This is an important issue, Ashley; does this capture the idea?" Joan asked as she continued to make a few notes on the easel. Ashley indicated that it did. "Does anyone else have another issue that they would like to present?"

"I do," stated Marlene, a member of the parent advisory council. "I'm not sure I represent all parents on this—and I'll help to find out—but I know that when my son has a long-term project I tend to get involved. I wish he had more of these opportunities, and I think longer periods of time would allow this type of learning to occur more often."

"These last few statements have helped me understand what has been bothering me. Block scheduling is a solution, not a problem. What *is* the problem here?" asked Robert. The room fell silent for several seconds.

"The problem is time," ventured Carol. "Perhaps our real challenge is to connect time and learning—maybe time *for* learning." The body language in the room seemed to confirm Carol's interpretation.

"I couldn't agree more," reflected Bill. "I think that 'time for learning' is the issue here. How do we best proceed with this problem statement?"

"To 'proceed' for us has come to mean an inquiry and protocol process. Is that what you have in mind, Bill?"

"Absolutely. Our research committee can help with the design, and our action research teams can get it underway over the next few weeks."

"Jose, you are chairing the research committee this year," Joan observed. "What is your response to where we are with this problem right now?"

"I can agree that 'time for learning' is the issue and the critical question as well. But it's a tough one. This isn't the first attempt—or the first school—to tackle the time issue. I think it would be helpful to the committee if all of us could take a few minutes to identify the most essential questions for the interviews and focus groups, visitations, and literature review," suggested Jose.

"That makes good sense," said Joan. She asked the faculty to talk with each other in small groups for 10 minutes. After the small-group dialogues, she asked the faculty to brainstorm a few questions. "John, would you help me to record some of our ideas? If time for learning is the issue, what are the questions? Let's focus especially on the student's perspective."

The staff came up with these questions for students:

- Do you have time to learn?
- Are there any activities that you now do in class that you do not have adequate time to finish?
- Are there learning experiences that you feel might strengthen your learning if you had more time to do them?
- What are the advantages and disadvantages to seeing fewer teachers and fewer students per day?
- If you had more time in class, what would that mean to you?
- Are there classes that you believe need to meet every day?
- What are some disadvantages of longer time blocks?

The staff decided to adapt these questions for focus groups that would include themselves and parents. Further, these questions would guide other forms of inquiry, including visits to other schools with different time schedules and the reading of articles and reports that chronicled the experiences and insights of others.

"This is a good start. The research committee meets tomorrow afternoon," commented Jose. "We should be able to give you some research guidelines by Friday."

"Would it be possible to report back our initial findings at our first meeting in February?" Heads nodded in general assent. "Okay," said Joan, "let's keep each other informed along the way. Any other business for today?"

During the intervening weeks, the research committee designed and guided an investigation process that involved interviewing a random sample of students; conducting focus groups of students, parents, and teachers; visitations to other schools using alternative schedules; and a review of the literature.

All faculty and representatives of students and parents worked in action research teams, each taking responsibility for a portion of the study. Each team was asked to begin by surfacing their expectations, assumptions, and beliefs about what they would discover. The staff members found that their expectations tended to follow subject lines. The perceived demands of the subject often influenced how faculty thought about time. Parents and students in the teams had fewer initial expectations—and their expectations tended to be different from those of the faculty. These conversations enabled team members to understand a fuller range of beliefs and expectations.

Faculty and administrators also shared responsibility for maintaining the focus of the dialogue, talking with each other in pairs and small groups, with students in classes, with parents in conferences, and in the short times and small spaces during which they saw each other informally. The principal assumed the role that he had sought for himself: out of the middle of the arena of action, supporting and guiding, using language that helped focus the agenda. The effect of all of these efforts was a concentrated consciousness about the issue of time and learning. By the time the whole staff met again, there was heightened awareness and specificity about this notion of "time for learning."

Faculty conversation II: Discussing preliminary findings

Six weeks later, Joan convened the faculty to discuss the findings of the first phase of inquiry about time for learning. Joan and the leadership team had designed a process for the faculty meeting that they hoped would integrate the findings and allow for maximum dialogue. The design had four components: (1) action research teams sharing some of their reflections on what they had expected to find when they began this process (these conversations had been held in the teams); (2) presentation of their findings so far, including four to six synthesized points; (3) dialogue about the interpretations and implications of these findings; and (4) next steps. The faculty had been notified of this process—one with which they were fairly familiar—ahead of time so that they could be prepared.

"All right," declared Jane at the start of the meeting. "Let's hear some of the findings."

Joan asked each action research team to report their key findings. As often occurred at times like this, the data decorated the room. Common themes began to emerge as participants noticed the relationship among findings. As they examined the evidence, Joan continued the dialogue by asking, "How do we make sense of this?"

"If I had to summarize what I see," observed Malcolm, "it might go something like this: Students say they learn best with long-term projects that they work on with other students and with the guidance of teachers. Parents seem to confirm that perception."

"Ummm," reflected Sally, "that does capture some central ideas for me as well, and I think it is a tribute to some of the instructional changes we've made—but it makes me ask, if we are accomplishing this within our current organization of time, why change?"

"I think that's a valid question, Sally, but the data suggest concerns as well. For instance, there is a persistent finding that students and teachers don't feel they have enough time to do justice to long-term projects, major concepts that cross subject matter lines, and preparation for exhibitions. During my visit to Granada High, I learned that these had been concerns for them as well, and were part of the reason for shifting to block scheduling."

"Another theme seems to relate to 'relationships,'" noted Jose. "Students, parents, and teachers spoke of the value of relating to fewer people for longer periods of time. We have had several conversations about the value of relationships—that's a high priority for us."

"The data are powerful," admitted Carol, "yet I notice that several points indicated that there were subjects that needed more frequent practice. I would also suggest that there are such subjects—particularly math and foreign languages."

"How frequent, Carol? How often would these classes need to meet? And are there different forms that these meetings could take?"

"What do you mean by different forms?" asked Carol.

"Well, perhaps longer periods with shorter seminars before or after school. Independent study groups during periods when formal class sessions are not scheduled. Open time in the language or math lab. Community service that provides unique opportunities for practice," offered Margery.

"Some of these different forms seemed to work well in the school where I did my internship," ventured Jefferson, a new teacher on the staff.

"How did that work, Jefferson?" asked Joan.

"For instance," Jefferson began, attracting the attention of the whole room, "some of the foreign language students performed community service with an active Latino community. This provided a lot of practice. The math class took on a long-term project that involved working with a development company that was building a new subdivision. I worked with that project. It was very exciting."

Eyes turned to Carol, who was clearly intrigued. "Interesting," she acknowledged. "But if we make some major changes here, I would like your commitment to work with us to design alternative approaches so that we can interact with students a minimum of three times a week."

"Agreed," declared Jose and Bill, almost in unison.

"I'd like to pose an additional question," stated Jeff, another member of the student leadership group. "If we have longer periods of time, and fewer of them, will I be able to complete all of my requirements for the university?"

"Who would like to respond to that?" asked Joan.

"I think I can," said Thomas, one of the original participants in the network meeting on block scheduling. "Jeff, let me give you an example. Currently you earn one unit for one year of English. Under a block schedule, one semester of English would earn you one unit. Since you spend more time with more depth, you earn more credit."

"That makes sense," said Jeff. "Thanks." Thomas nodded.

"Reorganizing our time seems like the natural next step for us," declared Gina. "We've made important strides in most other restructuring areas."

"I would tend to agree, Gina," began Catherine, a parent of a senior. "I have witnessed important changes at our school. And I would suggest another question that we regularly ask ourselves: 'How will we know if students are learning better?'"

"I'd like to suggest that Catherine's evaluation question and the evidence that we have discussed mean that we are ready to set criteria for how we will organize our time," commented the principal, Bill. "Criteria will help us choose the scheduling plans that best suit our needs as well as suggest the monitoring and evaluation strategies that need to be developed."

"How many of you feel as Bill does?" asked Joan. General nodding around the room. "I think I sense agreement? All right, I'd like to suggest that our next meeting be devoted to establishing criteria for the uses of time for learning. We'll have these notes typed up and distributed so that you can read them more closely and form some tentative suggestions before then."

Informal faculty conversation: Reflecting and processing

The third conversation took place right after the faculty meeting described previously. A small group of staff has stopped off for coffee on the way home. The group includes Joan, the faculty chair; Dick, a history teacher; Gina, a counselor; Mary, the community services coordinator; Carol, a math teacher; John, a foreign language teacher;

Jose, the chair of the research committee; and Martha, the vice principal.

After the orders were placed, John was eager to talk. "You know, on days like this—and we've had a few now—I feel a surge of professional pride! Frankly, I never thought we could be so civil and mindful at the same time. Your leadership has helped a lot, Joan."

"Thank you," said Joan, "but I can only take a small amount of the credit. Do you remember how this all got started?"

"I do!" exclaimed Gina. "When Bill was made principal, many of us thought, well, here is another district appointee sent to reform us. So we were especially surprised when, at the first meeting, he said, 'I don't know what the answers are, but we're going to talk about it and figure it out together.'"

"The first year and a half was pretty terrible," recalled John. "We seemed to accept our segregated, tracked classes, high absenteeism, and poor grades and to blame others for poor student achievement. We refused to look inward."

"Yet there was a turning point—just before Christmas of the second year when the race riot ended with serious injuries to Bobby Franklin. Ann looked us all in the eye and asked, 'Are we going to do anything about the conditions here that divide us—that are pulling us apart?'"

"I felt a shift in my thinking," acknowledged Jose. "I knew I could not continue to look the other way. And I doubt if it could have happened if we hadn't gone through a year of talking, struggling, and confronting our own practices and attitudes."

"After a soul-searching winter break," said Joan, "several of us agreed to take specific leadership roles, and many more of us agreed to learn the skills it would take to lead us out of the hole we'd been in for so long. By February, we'd agreed on some new goals and new processes—how we would work together."

"When I was hired by the faculty committee that spring," reflected Martha, "you were very clear about how this school worked. I was excited to be a part of it. And I haven't been disappointed."

"During those next three and a half years," Carol reminded her colleagues, "we trained ourselves in leadership skills, especially communication, dialogue, and inquiry, and joined the Coalition. We have detracked the school—without district mandate, I'd like to point out—altered our teaching strategies, and made a strong beginning in authentic assessment and the use of exhibitions. It is certainly time to do something with our crazy schedule. It just doesn't fit our needs anymore."

"The school-to-work programs and community service are especially strong—and, of course, they will be strengthened by longer time periods," commented Mary. "And as long as we are continually evaluating our work and fine-tuning it, we will continuously improve. I am convinced of it."

"But we can never become complacent or overconfident," warned Joan. "Many good schools go by the wayside if they are not vigilant. We have lots of challenges before us, not just the time problem that we're wrestling with now."

Capricorn and the Critical Features of High Leadership Capacity

Capricorn High School is an example of a school with high leadership capacity situated in Quadrant 4 of the Leadership Capacity Matrix (see Figure 2.1). Initially the principal, Bill Johnson, used his authority to convene and continue the conversation, a process that eventually broke through the traditional blaming and avoiding stance of many staff. As we joined the story, Bill had become a colleague and facilitator—making process observations and asking critical questions. He is not the primary actor in this drama.

Teachers, parents, students, and community members held significant leadership roles in the school. In addition to their new roles, their participation involved skillful dialogue, inquiry, reflection, and problem solving behavior. The flow of information was open, fluid, and complex, involving multiple forms of personal, small-group, and large-group interactions. Further, these participants discovered and created information through their habitual use of inquiry and innovation. Those involved took collective responsibility for the learning of all students. Predictably, student achievement was already high and improving among all groups.

The major challenge for Capricorn, as we shall see, is whether they can sustain their improvements.

Broad-based, skillful participation in the work of leadership

A majority of the Capricorn staff have become skillful leaders. Their resolve to improve their school has led to greater participation, peer observation and coaching, visitations to other schools, networking and regional conferences, and training. Students and parents are involved in every team and initiative; leadership skills are growing strong within both groups. In the above story, note the importance of parent and student contributions, and the respect extended to them by the faculty. Experience with the work of leadership has shifted attitudes and perspectives from passivity to active engagement, from blame to responsibility, and from cynicism to hopefulness.

Capricorn has a strong acculturation program for new teachers as well as for new students, parents, and administrators. Such acculturation is a concerted effort to enable newcomers to hit the road running—to understand how Capricorn works and the expectations it holds for new community members. Acculturation includes careful selection processes; orientation and assignment of a mentor educator, student, or family; and after-school or evening training sessions in leadership skills and understandings. It also means granting early and full participation in the process—a commitment that enables a young teacher like Jefferson to feel comfortable making contributions.

Inquiry-based use of information to inform shared decisions and practice

The staff at Capricorn use a schoolwide collaborative action research model in their cycle of improvement. They believe that everyone, not just individuals or small elite groups, needs to be involved. The learning process involves reflection, inquiry, dialogue, and action—as is evident in the story above.

Decision making and practice are both informed by the information emerging from the inquiry process as well as by an open and fluid flow of information from within and outside the school. A complex feedback loop that works a little like a "phone tree" of small dialogues is complemented by e-mail and written communications, miniconversations focused on the agenda at hand, and involvement in networks beyond the school.

Roles and responsibilities that reflect broad involvement and collaboration

Roles are blended and complementary as well. Much like a holograph, each person sees—or seeks to understand—the "whole picture" (an understanding of what the school is trying to accomplish and how the parts fit together into a systemic whole). Roles are defined by the needs of the students and the broader school community. Teachers serve as mentors and coaches to each other and to students and parents.

Notice that the Capricorn principal, Bill, aimed his comments primarily at synthesizing the position of the group, encouraging momentum or action, and making process suggestions. His role at this point is primarily one of "guardian of the process," but he also uses his influence as a catalyst for action. Bill doesn't show up as a dominant figure in the story, but in reality he constantly spoke to individuals and small groups, distributed articles, and ran interference with the district office. The principal and other administrators serve as learning facilitators, mediators, and ombudsmen. They model leadership behaviors, particularly by asking critical questions, convening dialogue sessions, and focusing the agenda. If the school's mission or values are seriously threatened, however, the principal is ready to play a more directive role. Authority and resources are redistributed so that teachers, students, and parents often act as entrepreneurs, taking responsibility for seeing an idea through to its conclusion.

Roles at Capricorn are also fluid. One can move in and out of active leadership without condemnation. For instance, a teacher who feels the need to ease back on her responsibilities will notify her colleagues of her intentions: "I am working on sharpening my skills in coaching student exhibitions, serving on our network team, and supporting my own son through his senior year of high school. I don't think I can serve on the research team this semester, but I'll be more active again in the fall."

Staff as a whole take responsibility for the implementation and evaluation of community decisions, participation in professional development, and engagement in the additional work of leading a community of learners.

Partly because there are some influential teacher association members at Capricorn, the association has avoided an oppositional stance in relation to changing roles and expectations there. However, because Capricorn is leading the reform efforts in this district, association members are feeling conflicted about the differing demands among schools (including some opposition to shared decision making). So far, association members have treated Capricorn as "the gifted child" (a special school with unique, nontransferable qualities), allowing it to move out ahead while being monitored carefully.

The role of the district and board is still limited in terms of capacity to support the work at Capricorn. Striving hard to maintain coherence and equality among schools, district personnel seem at times to stifle creativity and school initiative—to sacrifice innovation in pursuit of sameness. They still need to develop a range of support structures for schools in different stages of development. Unless the district can redefine its roles, the fate of Capricorn will remain uncertain as competition among schools threatens its existence.

Reflective practice/innovation as the norm

The processes in effect at Capricorn have, as we have seen, become second nature: "This is how we do things around here." Collegial professional development plans have replaced most aspects of traditional teacher evaluation (although the teachers and administrators still fill out the old forms together and send them in). These professional development plans involve collaborative planning and interactive learning, including peer coaching.

A natural outgrowth of the reflection, inquiry, and dialogue processes is innovation tied to the unique context of the school. The participants have invented innovations such as using the same coaching processes with students and adults. A special advisory program has now been linked to career mentoring and is sustained throughout the students' four years at the high school. The school and local university have initiated a plan to teach university classes on campus during the junior and senior years. And because they made sense to this school community, some innovations that took root are those that have become known as best practice in the profession: constructivist teaching, community service, student exhibitions.

High student achievement

Students are achieving well at Capricorn. Over the past three years, standardized test scores have risen, most markedly among ethnic/minority males. Evidence of self-direction is strong. Students are proactively forming learning plans, outlining and completing exhibitions, locating community sites in which to provide service, initiating relationships and requests for assistance, and assisting other students with their work.

Student leadership is formally evidenced on the ad hoc action research teams, the community council, the leadership team, the student council, and at the faculty meetings. Attendance and behavior problems are still present, although significantly decreased. Ninth grade transition and performance remain below what the school would hope for, and this issue has become a critical improvement target for students, parents, and staff.

Strategies for Sustaining High Leadership Capacity

Although Capricorn still has room to grow, its most interesting challenge is the sustainability of the processes and programs that warrant its recognition as a school with high leadership capacity. One major threat to sustainability has been superbly addressed: the capacity of Capricorn for self-renewal is not the sole possession of a few people or one principal. Leadership is broad based and skillful. The school will not crumple if a few key individuals leave.

Nevertheless, Capricorn faces two major sustainability issues: (1) sustaining the energy and commitment of staff who are actively involved in the school, and (2) avoiding the danger of "implosion" caused by a district, a teachers association, and a broader community that are not yet at the same stage of development as Capricorn.

The staff and community of Capricorn have identified the following approaches and strategies designed to address these two issues and sustain their accomplishments at the school. They have undertaken several of these—they cannot all be undertaken at once—and will phase in others.

The Capricorn school community will attend to their own development by continually reflecting upon their own processes and progress. They will keep scheduled time and an organizational structure for reflection, inquiry, and dialogue. And this cycle of inquiry will prove to be a boon when the periodic program accreditation occurs. The school community members keep their histomap up-to-date for all to see and have begun a school portfolio to chronicle their progress. They created the histomap in a whole-staff meeting; the librarian and a subcommittee of the leadership team manage the portfolio process.

Capricorn will stop accepting the "gifted child status" and direct substantial influence toward feeder schools, universities, other schools in the district, district personnel, associations, professional organizations, and community agencies. By seeking to create a more congruent context for themselves and to receive broader feedback, they will be able to strengthen other educational institutions as well as their own.

The Capricorn school community will reach out to the district and the teachers association in the following ways:

• Compose new role descriptions for Capricorn staff and present them to the district, teachers association, and board personnel; include a clear accountability system as a part of shared responsibility; mediate these discussions with all concerned; request that the school board accept the report.

• Propose a comprehensive hiring policy that is inclusive and heavily school-based; generate early collaboration and support from other schools and associations.

• Request at a principals meeting and teachers association meeting that a new teacher evaluation task force be formed; ensure ample participation from Capricorn teachers.

• Suggest to both the associations and the district that site-based management be written into the certificated and classified contracts with the district.

Capricorn will approach the local university that provides most of its student and intern teachers to explore the establishment of a Professional Development School. This practice can significantly extend the influence of the school into the university and vice versa, ensuring that candidates are well prepared to assume responsible roles.

They will arrange for staff to secure training in advanced coaching strategies to strengthen their listening and questioning skills with students and each other as well as to prepare them for the mediative challenges described above. These mediative challenges involve communication, conflict management, and the ability to create new solutions out of differing points of view.

They will develop professional products and publications such as dialogue guides, professional development plans, position papers, workshop agendas, and journal articles in order to share and disseminate the work at Capricorn.

They will blend established practices with process modifications in order to keep the work vibrant, not routine. For instance, they will sharpen dialogue, inquiry, and reflection processes by adding new skills and strategies; they will meet off campus. Occasionally, they will secure an outside facilitator, hold a dinner or breakfast meeting.

Finally, Capricorn will not lose its student focus. Because children, families, and society are always changing, so must a school.

A Few Afterthoughts

Traditionally, high schools contend with a number of elements that mitigate against systemic improvement. These mitigating elements include organizational structure, size, athletic programs, and the narrow professional preparation of high school teachers. The structure is compartmentalized and organized around a hierarchical authority arrangement. Large school size means that relationships are difficult to attend to. The demands of athletic programs drain attention and energy away from important issues of teaching and learning. Teachers are prepared to teach disciplines, not students.

Capricorn High School was able to overcome these obstacles through persistent professional dialogue that enabled staff to challenge old assumptions and reawaken their fundamental need to care about their students and their own worth. This process required a faculty of professional educators who stayed with the process long enough to learn some new ways of doing business and a principal with a capacity to use authority to convene and support the dialogue rather than to give the answers and commands. Everyone learned that real change requires the development of new skills, inquiry, program modification, compromise, and time.

These undertakings add up to considerable change for the better in conditions for students, parents, and staff. Unless a school is starting from the ground up with a highly prepared staff, increasing leadership capacity over time is the most productive way to bring about improvements that can be sustained.

ESSENTIAL ACTIONS FOR BUILDING LEADERSHIP CAPACITY IN YOUR SCHOOL AND DISTRICT

IN THE LAST THREE CHAPTERS, THE STORIES OF THREE SCHOOLS set forth the major issues and dilemmas inherent in building leadership capacity in schools. The approaches and strategies were tailored to those specific situations, although most of them hold value for all schools.

But how do you get started on building leadership capacity? What are the basic actions that all districts and schools should undertake to engage in this work? This chapter sets forth a few useful guidelines—not a 5- or 10-step plan, but a set of actions that educators need to take if leadership capacity is to grow. Your district may already be taking some of these actions; others will need your explicit attention. Use these guidelines to help you decide where and how to proceed.

Keep in mind that these guidelines are systemic. That is, they are connected in such a way that they form a dynamic relationship to each other and to the set. If some essential actions are missing, others will become dysfunctional. However, these actions are not narrowly prescriptive. For instance, you can hire personnel well suited for the work at hand, but you must invest heavily in professional development, as well. Any number of governance structures will work—what is important is the breadth and skillfulness of involvement. There are multiple strategies for inquiry and problem solving; you will want to choose those best suited to your school and your staff.

Taking Action to Build Leadership Capacity

1. Hire personnel with the capacity to do leadership work

District personnel procedures often rely too heavily upon paper screening and interviews to select principals, teachers, and other employees. These procedures—even when the interview panel is broadly representative of the community—are notoriously unreliable. This is particularly true if the goal is to hire collaborative, inclusive individuals who possess some of the fundamental perspectives and skills needed to participate actively in building leadership capacity in schools and districts.

An increasingly frequent practice used in the selection of teachers calls for the candidates to teach a lesson, with trained observers looking for indicators of effective instructional skills. Many districts are using simulations to judge how well teacher candidates can coach or work in a group. In addition to assessing a demonstration lesson, it can be powerful to observe teacher candidates interact with each other in a problem-solving activity; respond to a case study about a dilemma with parents and children; and describe how they perceive their role as teachers, how they improve their craft, and what curiosities drive their interests. The goal here is to find teachers who view themselves as responsible to the school community and the profession, as well as to the classroom.

I would strongly urge further use of the assessment center concept by asking administrative candidates to demonstrate dialogue facilitation (watch for engagement without dominance); case study analysis and strategy description (such as found in Chapters 3 through 5); the capacity to listen, mediate, and coach; and the ability to compose a clear, visionary statement to the community. Interviews are still essential, but as only one aspect of the assessment process. Paper screening remains a prerequisite procedure, although it is vital that panels be sensitive to nontraditional career paths that may serve as excellent preparation for professional roles. Because white males have had more opportunities to perform in leadership roles, women and minority candidates can get lost in the paper screening process. If a district uses more comprehensive assessment activities, it needs to worry less about an improper selection—there will be ample information available to make an outstanding choice.

In the assessment and selection of new personnel, keep in mind that certain dispositions or perspectives in candidates increase the likelihood of staffing a school with the potential for high leadership capacity. These dispositions or perspectives include the following:

- A constructivist philosophy of learning (although the candidates may not use the term)
- A view of themselves as being responsible for all of the students in the school
- A willingness to participate in decision making
- A readiness to work together to accomplish the school's goals
- An understanding of how they can learn to improve their own craft

Before the final selection decision, district and school expectations need to be clarified for the candidate. An example that remains strong in my memory occurred in 1969 when I became a new teacher at Bell Junior High School in Golden, Colorado. The principal, George Carnie, explained to me that working there meant that I would share in the leadership of the school and that during my first semester I would be required to take a 30-hour workshop—in the evening—to gain skills in the four areas or principles upon which the school was built: shared decision making, open communication, problem solving, and accountability. Needless to say, this experience influenced me greatly as a young teacher and later as a principal.

Whether or not a district has the luxury to hire many new personnel, it is essential that all staff be afforded ample opportunities for professional development, mentoring support, coaching, inquiry, serving in leadership roles, and networking. District and school personnel need to be able to grow and develop together rather than see the infusion of new blood as a panacea for tired systems.

2. Get to know one another

You will have noticed in previous examples that I give a great deal of importance to building trusting environments with solid relationships. We need to know each other as whole individuals: as colleagues, friends, parents, citizens. It is through these relationships that we can understand and respect each other's experiences, values, and aspirations. Within such authentic relationships, our self-concepts and world views nestle and evolve. We can make public and discuss our fundamental beliefs when we know we can count on others to respect us for who we are, regardless of our differences. This is a tall order in any organization, but it is vital in schools because we expect educators to form such relationships with students, as well.

Authentic relationships are fostered by personal conversations, frequent dialogue, shared work, and shared responsibilities. As individuals interact with one another, they tend to listen across boundaries—boundaries erected by disciplines, grade levels, expertise, authority, position, race, and gender. In Action 5 (see p. 83), one of the criteria for selecting governance and work structures is to maximize interactions that allow for relationship building.

Trust is built and experienced within the context of multifaceted communication systems such as those described earlier in this book. A communication system needs to be open and fluid, include feedback loops, and be practiced by everyone in the school. The central function of such a system is to create and share information and to interpret and make sense of information as it is generated and shared. Rumor is a persistent communication disrupter in most schools; assertive information sharing can disarm rumor mills.

I am not suggesting, however, that we wait to know each other well before getting on with the work of schooling. We can build relationships before we begin new work, but the relationships primarily develop as we move toward a shared purpose of schooling.

3. Assess staff and school capacity for leadership

Building leadership capacity is primarily a function of the five critical features of schools described in previous chapters:

- Broad-based, skillful participation in the work of leadership
- Inquiry-based use of information to inform shared decisions and practice
- Roles and responsibilities that reflect broad involvement and collaboration
- Reflective practice/innovation as the norm
- High student achievement

The dispositions, knowledge, and skills essential to the achievement of these features are learned in a variety of ways: by observation and reflection, modeling and metacognition (the facilitator/coach talks aloud about the process strategies in use), guided practice, collaborative work, and training. Learning that is embedded in the work itself is far more powerful than decontextualized training (unless the faculty itself says, for example, "We are stuck here, and we need some training in the use of consensus").

A listing of the needed dispositions, knowledge, and skills appears in the Leadership Capacity Staff Survey in Appendix A.[1] This survey

---

[1] A Rubric of Emerging Teacher Leadership appears in Appendix C.

is useful for an entire faculty, a leadership team, or other small groups. Before completing the survey, staff members need to understand the source of the ideas and the concept of leadership capacity so they have a context for understanding and responding to the survey items. Further, this survey can be used in conjunction with the Leadership Capacity School Survey in Appendix B. Administering the two surveys at the same time can be a useful way for staff to weigh their skills in relation to school needs and expectations.

It is helpful to have each individual complete the staff survey with one or two trusted colleagues. Work in groups of three, asking each person to complete his or her own survey and surveys for the two other individuals. Talk through the results, looking for agreements and discrepancies. Discuss the discrepancies, asking for examples that influenced the responses. This "triangulated" feedback can be a powerful learning experience for staff and can lead to genuine commitments to skill building.

Once the survey is administered and self-scored, the results have implications for individual professional development plans and schoolwide professional development. A wall chart that summarizes the staff's three or four highest needs can create a pattern and direction for staff learning—including staff training. It can also serve as a decision-making tool to help staff select among options for participation. For instance, "Am I prepared to serve on the leadership team, research group, an ad hoc action team? Chair a grade-level group? Organize a support group for new teachers? Serve as a process observer? A peer coach?"

4. Develop a culture of inquiry

A basic human learning need is to frame our work and our lives with big questions: How can I reach my students better? What really works? How will I define myself as a teacher, father, community member? A commitment to a culture of inquiry responds to this need by providing a forum in which we can surface and describe our most compelling questions. This culture is often not the norm in schools where teaching and learning have become technical and routine processes. When we pose questions of relevance, we reenergize ourselves and focus our work together.

In this pursuit, it is essential that the reciprocal processes of leadership—reflection, inquiry, dialogue, and action—be integrated into the daily patterns of life in schools. Many approaches and strategies are in use that establish these processes. A missing link in many such efforts is a constructivist necessity: to begin our inquiries by evoking our previous experiences, assumptions, values, and beliefs about the issues at hand. Doing this makes it more likely that we will be able to pose relevant questions and mediate new learnings.

One of the most comprehensive inquiry approaches is what is known as whole school and collaborative action research. It is "comprehensive" in that it aims at whole school improvement while building collaborative inquiry habits of mind. In addition to action research, the following strategies are effective in building a culture of inquiry:

- Use of the dialogue protocol (see Chapter 4) to shape and refine new practices and to examine student work
- Work sessions for examining and assessing student work
- Peer coaching and peer review
- Collective problem-solving strategies that include finding problems, posing alternative actions, monitoring, and evaluating
- Other forms of research such as reviews of the literature, Internet searches and chat rooms, visits to other schools, and attendance at network meetings and conferences
- Examination of disaggregated data (breaking performance data down by gender, race, socioeconomic status, ethnicity, disabilities) and such other readily available school data as attendance, suspensions, expulsions, standardized scores.
- Grounding work in the school's vision while continually comparing practice and results with intentions: Is this what we planned?

Are we achieving what we had hoped? Are our children learning to read?

Each of these strategies has its own strengths. Choices are guided by the questions you have to answer, your priorities, the roles and structures that you've established, and the skillfulness of the staff. Some of these strategies should be initially undertaken with technical assistance. Most schools are expected to participate in an external program review or accreditation process, usually involving a self-study. The school that has developed its own culture of inquiry will find these external reviews easy to accommodate; the reviews will become simply a variant on their own inquiry processes.

5. Organize the school community for leadership work

To organize for leadership work means to establish structures, groups, and roles that serve as the infrastructure for the self-renewing processes of a culture of inquiry. Because each structure requires skillful participation, the staff and school assessment processes described above will inform the selection of groups and processes. Other questions to consider when designing school structures include the following:

- How will we make decisions at our school?
- How will we organize for reflection, inquiry, dialogue, and action?
- How will we maximize participation and interaction?
- How will the groups relate to each other?
- What forms of communication will create dense feedback loops among groups and individuals?
- How will the roles of group participants be described?
- What groups or individuals will participate in professional networks? How will ideas from those sources stimulate and inform the work within the school?

- How will we provide a forum for feedback to and from other schools, the district, organizations, and universities?

Answers to these guiding questions will focus the planning for school organization. Schools have found many working arrangements useful: leadership teams, facilitation teams or research teams (for guiding action research), ad hoc groups on various topics (school climate, advisory committee, care team, assessment task force), grade-level teams, interdisciplinary teams, school site councils, and school improvement councils.

Roles and responsibilities will emerge and be defined in reference to these structures and the purposes they serve. For instance, as teachers begin to view themselves as leaders, they will also take on the mantle of mentor, facilitator, coach, and mediator. University faculty, district or other school personnel, retired educators, or community members from other professions can be valued members of any of these groups. These partners can provide technical assistance; serve as an ombudsman, coach, mediator, or critical friend; or just offer an alternative perspective.

Although collaboration is key in school organization, it can also have its dark side. Collaboration, if used indiscriminately, can become burdensome and overwhelming. If used for every decision and action, individuals will spend all of their time going to meetings and everything will seem of equal importance. To focus on those things that really matter, it is helpful to have a structure for accomplishing work that is routine, or at least has been performed often enough that it has been finely tuned.

An example of such a strategy is called ZCI (for AuthoriZed, Consulted, and Informed). I have used it in more than a dozen settings over the past 20 years and found it to be useful in accomplishing major tasks beyond the boundaries of a meeting. ZCI is displayed in a matrix with the tasks to be accomplished recorded along the left-hand column. Across the top are three columns: Z, C, and I. This matrix creates boxes into which staff members place their names. Someone who has a Z on a task—for example, organizing open house—is "authoriZed" to assume the major responsibility for seeing that the work is completed. This person plans and consults with those listed in the C column, and informs those listed in the I column. I suggest that each faculty member agree to take on at least one Z during the course of the year. A principal will take a few Zs, but more often will serve as a C. This strategy, and others like it, can cushion the impact of extensive collaboration, accomplish the school's work efficiently, and protect the agenda for items of major importance.

One form of organization that needs to be coordinated with other schools, the district, parents and community, and professional organizations is the school calendar. The calendar should serve as a picture of the school's structure. Enter each group's meeting times on the calendar so that each member of the community will have a sense of the whole and opportunities to inform and influence the working groups. Think of the calendar as an X-ray of the school's arterial system, most healthy when it is unclogged and open.

6. Implement your plans for building leadership capacity

Many leaders in educational reform have helped us to recognize the developmental nature of implementation. This observation is particularly true in building leadership capacity, because the changes at hand are both personal and organizational. Educators, parents, and students are often required to alter their self-perceptions in order to perceive themselves as leaders. Redefining leadership can help tremendously. Individuals are more ready to view themselves as facilitators of learning for adults—a natural extension of their work with children—than as gurus or warriors on white horses.

These changing self-perceptions are necessarily accompanied by a redesigned pattern of organization for the school and district that allows the work of leadership to be carried out. This is difficult work, requiring persistence, patience, and deeply held beliefs about the capabilities of individuals and schools.

Persistence is "hanging in there" until the work is done, but it is a particular way of hanging in there. Persistence does not mean patiently waiting for people to "see the light." Rather, it entails listening, posing tough questions, describing, mediating, and surfacing and confronting conflict. When opposition occurs in the form of active resistance or passive aggressiveness, it is vital to ask about the source of the feelings, listen carefully, and enter into dialogue about the implications of these conflicting ideas. It is not useful to do a "hard sell." What is vital is to secure agreement to stay in the dialogue.

Because the work of building leadership capacity, like any important endeavor, is developmental, there will be indicators of progress at different stages of the journey. A few indicators that will tell you that you are making progress are the following:

- Listening to each other and building on each other's ideas
- Posing essential questions, whose answers will address the school's fundamental purpose
- Challenging and mediating resistance
- Encountering and solving problems—rather than only describing difficult conditions
- Visiting each other's classrooms and reflecting with each other on what you observe
- Transforming cynicism into hopefulness by transforming the school's most challenging issues into clear statements of purpose or inquiry
- Talking about teaching and learning in the faculty room
- Initiating innovative ideas and monitoring the progress of the innovation

For more indicators of progress, see columns 3 and 4 in the Rubric of Emerging Teacher Leadership in Appendix C.

Remember, leadership capacity is basically content free. That is, it is the fundamental work of schooling that accompanies any reform effort—improving literacy, instruction, assessment, school restructuring, parent participation. To implement any innovation successfully requires strengthening the leadership capacity of the school.

7. Develop district policies and practices that support leadership capacity building

When values, policies, and practices are applied to the system as a whole—the whole school district—schools tend toward self-renewal. However, when school districts attempt to apply rules to schools as isolated units, the system as a whole tends toward imbalance and disorder. Once districts become effective, schools can function with a great deal of autonomy within those frameworks established collaboratively by the district as a whole. Effective schools within ineffective districts tend to be idiosyncratic, isolated happenstances, not often sustainable (consider the journey of Capricorn High, discussed in Chapter 5).

An "effective district" capable of building and supporting leadership capacity in all of its schools aligns its policies and practices with a coherent set of values, such as the assumptions about leadership described in Chapter 1. Although it is not possible in this space to discuss all features of district effectiveness, a few key features follow.

Relationships with schools that involve two correlates: high engagement and low bureaucratization. High engagement means frequent interaction and two-way communication, mutual coordination and reciprocal influence, and some shared goals and objectives. Low bureaucratization means an absence of extensive rules and regulations governing the relationship (Louis, 1989). Such engagement takes on a mediative quality: mediating relationships among schools and in regional networks, creating feedback loops, disseminating ideas, and securing broad-based participation. Access to district personnel is open and nonhierarchical.

Shared decision making at the district level; major decentralization of authority and resources to schools through site-based management. This relationship necessitates shared accountability that involves complementary district and school site plans for improvement and accountability. Linda Darling-Hammond (1993) points out that effective accountability requires that schools organize themselves so that students will not fall through the cracks, create means for continual collegial inquiry, and use authority responsibly to make necessary changes. Districts must also organize in these ways, particularly with regard to redistributing authority to and among schools and educators.

A sharp focus on student and adult learning. District agendas, goal statements, and communications with personnel and with the community and professional organizations need to use consistent language that captures the district vision about student and adult learning. Policies and practices need to be congruent with instructional and assessment practices. For instance, teacher and administrator assessment needs to be aligned with performance-based student assessment and to focus on learning more than on strictly evaluative measures. Learning-based approaches to teacher and administrator assessment include choices among alternative paths for assessment, guided self-assessment, collegial coaching and review, and portfolios. Assessment criteria include collegial and leadership performance. Professional development needs to be defined as opportunities to learn, rather than as training. "Opportunities to learn" means engagement in shared decision making, inquiry, dialogue, reflection, community service, peer coaching and mediation, workshops. To lead is to facilitate such learning toward a shared purpose.

Modeling the processes of a learning organization that are advocated for schools in Actions 1 through 6 of this chapter. Appropriate personnel selection, relationship building, leadership assessment, a culture of inquiry, and an organization that promotes broad-based, skillful leadership are as essential for the district as for the school. See the School District Personnel Practice and Policies document in Appendix D.

These four arenas of district work frame the "leading-supporting" role essential for effective districts. Through reciprocal engagement with schools focused on vision, purpose, and relationships—rather than rules, rigid procedures, and mandates—districts can become full educational partners with their communities.

The Basis for Building Leadership Capacity: Assumptions and Actions

Chapter 1 presents five assumptions that serve as the basic premises for building leadership capacity in schools and districts:

1. Leadership is not trait theory; leadership and leader are not the same.
2. Leadership is about learning.
3. Everyone has the potential and right to work as a leader.
4. Leading is a shared endeavor.
5. Leadership requires the redistribution of power and authority.

These assumptions provide the conceptual framework for taking the actions described in this chapter:

1. Hire personnel with the capacity to do leadership work.
2. Get to know one another.
3. Assess staff and school capacity for leadership.
4. Develop a culture of inquiry.
5. Organize the school community for leadership work.
6. Implement your plans for building leadership capacity.
7. Develop district policies and practices that support leadership capacity building.

Focusing on these five assumptions and taking these seven actions will build leadership capacity in your school and district. That doesn't mean that all of the needed perspectives, strategies, and "answers" are in this little book. Chapter 7 attempts to anticipate your questions by addressing those that are commonly asked in workshops. A few of the answers will add to your understandings. However, the greatest understandings will emerge in true constructivist fashion when you and your colleagues undertake this work together—and reflect collaboratively on what you experience and learn.

QUESTIONS AND A
FEW ANSWERS

THE PREVIOUS CHAPTERS SET FORTH THE IDEA OF BUILDING leadership capacity in schools and presented three examples of schools at different stages of development. Whenever a new concept enters our professional lives, no set of explanations can satisfy all of our curiosities or answer all of our questions. Because we will each come to the idea with different experiences, assumptions, and perceptions, understandings will vary. This variance in understandings will be widened by the lack of opportunity for conversation. In this chapter, I have attempted to anticipate some of your questions. Many of these questions have been asked by participants in workshops, conversations, and classes. You may find some of your questions here, as well.

Once again, what do you mean by "leadership capacity"?

"Leadership capacity" refers to broad-based, skillful participation in the work of leadership. The work of leadership involves attention to shared learning that leads to shared purpose and action. In schools, increased leadership capacity means that the principal is one leader—

and a very important leader. But he or she does not fill all or even most of the leadership roles in the building.

How is leadership capacity different from shared decision making?

Shared decision making is one aspect of leadership capacity. But learning in schools is about more than decisions. It is about our daily work together—reflection, dialogue, inquiry, and action. This work involves new roles and responsibilities that reframe all of our interactions together, not just those at decision points.

You've chosen five critical features of leadership capacity. Why these five?

These five features (broad-based, skillful participation; inquiry-based use of information to inform decisions and practice; roles and responsibilities that reflect broad involvement and collaboration; reflective practice and innovation as the norm; high student achievement) are firmly tied to school improvement and student achievement. You may have recognized that the fifth feature, high student achievement, is both a dimension of collaborative work (teaching and learning for children) and an outcome. Together, these features form a dynamic relationship; no one or two features will result in high leadership capacity or high student achievement. It is a case of the sum being greater than the parts.

Is the goal that every educator become a leader? If so, why?

Yes. Leaders are perceived as consummate learners who attend to the learning of both adults and children—including themselves, of course. This is what it should mean to be a professional educator. It does not mean that all leadership work will look the same. While some educators will chair committees and facilitate large-group meetings, others will focus their energies on implementing peer coaching, team teaching, conducting collaborative action research, and demonstrating reflective practice.

Some teachers do not see themselves as leaders—and do not want to see themselves as leaders. How do I work with them?

By redefining leadership as constructivist learning, teachers are more able to find this work congruent with their work with children. Some teachers will take on several leadership roles; other may wish to accept fewer or more modest roles or tasks. In a setting that encourages leadership, it is a rare teacher who will entirely resist this opportunity.

Why do you insist on using the therapeutic term "codependency" in reference to relationships in school?

Codependency refers to dependence on one another to reinforce immature roles and uses of power and authority. It is an apt term for the entangled, traditional relationships in schools that have kept educators from growing. Without broad-based leadership, the ability of a school to grow and become better for children is limited.

We know a lot about how children learn. Why can't we just implement what we know?

We haven't been able to implement what we know. Sometimes, going from A to B is not the shortest route. We now know that unless teachers are learning together, they will not be able to create engaging learning experiences for children. Using that understanding will open a door and allow many other ideas and skills to be implemented.

Is there a tension between inquiry and innovation?

Yes. Genuine inquiry tends to produce home-grown solutions. Innovation sometimes means finding a good program elsewhere and inserting it into the school. Best practices that have been carefully researched can be very useful to a school. When inquiry leads a school to realize what is needed, a survey of promising practices can produce a program that is well suited for the school. Broad leadership allows the administration and faculty to blend, adapt, and adjust practices to fit that particular school.

Our school is considered successful, yet minority students are doing poorly. Where do we start?

You start by having a thoughtful dialogue among school community members (including parents) to understand the current situation. This dialogue needs to consider the disaggregated data that led to the conclusion that minority students were not doing well. Participants will need to confront their own assumptions about which groups of students can learn and under what circumstances they learn best. The next step is to work on the practical tasks that will make the school truly successful. (Chapters 3–5 contain some suggestions.)

How does all of this fit in with the movement toward a standards-driven system?

As I have noted, leadership capacity is an essential element of any reform. The key issue with a standards-driven system is how the standards were devised and who decides how they are to be implemented. Standards that are collaboratively designed and implemented by using (1) the expert knowledge of school staff and community members and (2) the findings of best practice can evoke commitment and competence from all concerned. Even if the standards are externally imposed, the school staff can determine how they will be applied or adapted in that school's particular situation.

Why are changing roles so central to the work of building leadership capacity?

Changing roles grow out of changing self-perceptions; and, in turn, new roles provide "spaces" in which individuals can redefine what it is to be a teacher, parent, student, administrator. New roles are accompanied by new perspectives and responsibilities. As roles evolve, members of a school community reach a point of collective responsibility—a condition demonstrably linked to high student achievement.

What do you mean by "responsibility"?

I prefer the term "responsibility" to "accountability." Responsibility involves an internal commitment to self-improvement, the improvement of others around us, and the school community at large. Accountability, on the other hand, has tended to mean that we are being "held accountable" by some outside authority. Accountability measures often mitigate against the development of responsibility, because external demands can evoke compliance and resistance.

You've given a lot of attention to communication and information systems. Schools are closely knit places; can't we just talk with each other?

"Talking with each other" is often random, erratic, and dependent on personality. An information and feedback system needs to be consciously planned and implemented to ensure that frequency and quality of communication are more nearly the same for everyone. "Quality" here refers to respectful listening, asking essential questions, giving and receiving specific feedback.

I think I'm an effective teacher (and my principal and colleagues seem to agree), but I work best by myself. How will I fit into the "new order"?

Adults, like children, have different preferred learning styles. It is important that learning alternatives exist that honor all styles. However, it is also important that adults work to expand their learning style repertoire in order to engage with all learners collectively. Part of the reason that I recommend results-oriented conversations is to attend to the frustration felt by some adults when they are caught up in open-ended discussions and conversations. As stated earlier, some teachers will accept more leadership responsibilities than others—and no teacher should be coerced into a role that makes him or her very uncomfortable.

With all of this involvement in the work of leading, isn't the classroom being neglected?

Because student achievement is firmly connected to the adult learning and leading behaviors recommended here, building leadership capacity is not a diversion but a necessity. It is also important to remember that expanding leadership roles takes two forms: (1) taking on additional tasks or functions and (2) behaving more skillfully in daily interactions (e.g., asking questions, listening, provoking, giving feedback). The latter form doesn't take more time; it merely reframes how we do what we already do.

Isn't there a danger in attempting so much involvement outside the school?

Well, yes. But there is a greater danger from too little involvement outside the school. Schools need to help create congruent contexts (user-friendly communities and districts) in which to function, broaden feedback loops for self-renewal, and develop opportunities for professional development. Isolated school environments contribute to ingrown, self-indulgent solutions. As educators develop, they naturally assume more responsibility for the broader community and the profession. Such expanding responsibilities will not occur if outside opportunities do not exist for each faculty member.

In a district that says to the principal, "The buck stops at your desk," do we have a chance at building high leadership capacity?

When a district uses a narrow, hierarchical approach to accountability, the work before you is much more difficult. A district needs to change its accountability system from being dependent on a person to being dependent on the school community. The establishment at each site of a broad-based inquiry system that will incorporate both self-evaluation and self-renewal is vital and complex (sometimes this is called "lateral accountability"). Yet, as we have seen in the Capricorn High School story, a school can go a long way toward shared responsibility if the principal is willing to make new roles and responsibilities explicit to all concerned.

Aren't you underplaying the role of the principal?

On the surface it may seem that way. Actually, as I noted in Chapter 2, the role of the principal in building leadership capacity is more demanding and complex than the old work of telling and directing. However, the principal now shares the spotlight with teachers, parents, students, and other community members—acting more as a choreographer than a prima ballerina.

You seem to be recommending that teachers become political mediators, right?

Teachers are already political mediators. By this I mean they seek to influence those in key decision-making roles in order to get things done. They influence the principal, curriculum directors, assistant superintendent and superintendent, parent community, school board, and community groups. When they don't find the means or mechanisms for doing this personally or in small groups, they may work through their unions or associations. Working in the classroom, the school, and the community involves working with information, power, persuasion, and influence. I am just suggesting that the mediation work become more focused and skillful . . . and collaborative.

What are the district policies that are critical for building leadership capacity?

Districts need to continually review policies to make sure those policies are truly supportive of the instructional program in classrooms and schools. Some guidelines for analyzing and testing policies appear in Appendix D. Underlying these guidelines is the conviction that school districts themselves must become constructivist learning communities—using, promoting, and facilitating the reciprocal proc- esses that are advocated for schools.

With broad-based leadership and collective responsibility, aren't superintendents and school boards losing control?

Yes, they are losing one form of control—the form that stifles sustainable development. A new form of control emerges, one that invests itself in learning and long-range results. This new form requires that superintendents and board members let go of the need for daily predictabilities, narrow objectives, the development of "knee-jerk" policies, self-indulgence in crisis, and a paternalistic stance. As I noted in Chapter 6, this is not to suggest a hands-off approach, but rather an approach characterized by high engagement and low bureaucratization. Superintendents and school boards play an important role in a district with high leadership capacity. They continue to provide oversight, they are even more involved in the life of the district, but they resist the temptation to impose quick change through top-down mandates and fiats.

We seem to spend a lot of energy "retraining" our teachers and administrators after their preparation in universities. Why can't university preparation programs be more effective in the first place?

Universities suffer from the same maladies as schools. Change is difficult. Adequate feedback systems for informing universities about their successes are rare. And there is no agreed-upon definition for "success." Many universities define success as the number of scholarly publications produced by faculty.

Among the most promising practices for colearning among insti- tutions is the Professional Development School. Further, universities can teach specific strategies, familiarize students with alternatives, evoke and support social justice values, and create the disposition for broad-based leadership.

What should be the role of universities with K–12 schools?

Both institutions desperately need external feedback loops that will improve the quality of programs in each. Because the Professional Development School is intended to focus on preparation of new educators and whole school change, there are many roles that faculty from schools and universities can fulfill. University faculty can serve as members of school research and development teams, site councils, and leadership teams and act as critical friends and coaches. In turn, the university needs to reframe entrance requirements for students, to host teachers as critical friends and visiting faculty, and to translate what they learn from schools into improved programs and curriculum.

This seems all too complicated. Can ordinary teachers and principals understand it and use it?

Never underestimate the capacity of people to understand and use ideas that are congruent with their desire for learning.

If we all take these ideas to heart and implement them, how soon will we have excellent schools?

If you focus your attention on building leadership capacity in schools, within 18 months you will notice major dispositional shifts among almost all involved. By the second year major structural changes will be underway. And by the end of the second year you should notice changes in student academic performance (improvements in social behavior will come earlier). Considering that the educational lore says that it takes 3 to 10 years to improve a school (and, of course, it does), building leadership capacity with constructivist strategies can be surprisingly efficient!

These are just a sampling of questions and issues that people might raise about the concept and practice of leadership capacity. Other provocative questions are posed in a Study Guide that is published on the ASCD Web site (http://www.ascd.org).

LEADERSHIP CAPACITY
STAFF SURVEY

This is an assessment of leadership dispositions, knowledge, and skills needed to build leadership capacity in schools and organizations. The items are clustered by the characteristics of schools with high leadership capacity. It may be completed by a school staff member or by a colleague who is familiar with the work of that staff member. The survey information is most useful if each staff member completes a survey as a self-assessment and then asks for an assessment by two colleagues. To the right of each item is a Likert-type scale:

NO = not observed

IP = infrequently performed

FP = frequently performed

CP = consistently performed

CTO = can teach to others

Please circle the rating for each item.

A. Broad-based participation in the work of leadership

1. Assists in the establishment of representative governance and work groups.	NO	IP	FP	CP	CTO
2. Organizes the school to maximize interactions among all school and community members.	NO	IP	FP	CP	CTO
3. Shares authority and resources broadly.	NO	IP	FP	CP	CTO
4. Engages others in opportunities to lead.	NO	IP	FP	CP	CTO
Total numbers	—	—	—	—	—

B. Skillful participation in the work of leadership

5. Models, describes, and demonstrates the following leadership skills:

a. develops shared purpose of learning;	NO	IP	FP	CP	CTO
b. facilitates group processes;	NO	IP	FP	CP	CTO
c. communicates (especially listening and questioning);	NO	IP	FP	CP	CTO
d. reflects on practice;	NO	IP	FP	CP	CTO
e. inquires into the questions and issues confronting your school community;	NO	IP	FP	CP	CTO
f. collaborates in planning;	NO	IP	FP	CP	CTO
g. manages conflict among adults;	NO	IP	FP	CP	CTO
h. problem solves with colleagues and students;	NO	IP	FP	CP	CTO

Note: NO = not observed; IP = infrequently performed; F = frequently performed; CP = consistently performed; CTO = can teach to others.

B. Skillful participation in the work of leadership—continued

	NO	IP	FP	CP	CTO
i. manages change and transitions;	NO	IP	FP	CP	CTO
j. uses constructivist learning designs for students and adults.	NO	IP	FP	CP	CTO
6. Communicates through action and words the relationship between leadership and learning.	NO	IP	FP	CP	CTO
Total numbers	—	—	—	—	—

C. Inquiry-based use of information to inform shared decisions and practice

	NO	IP	FP	CP	CTO
7. Engages with others in a learning cycle (reflection, dialogue, question posing, inquiry, construction of meaning, planned action).	NO	IP	FP	CP	CTO
8. Develops plans and schedules for the creation of shared time for dialogue and reflection.	NO	IP	FP	CP	CTO
9. Identifies, discovers, and interprets information and school data/evidence.	NO	IP	FP	CP	CTO
10. Designs and implements a communication system that keeps all informed and involved in securing and interpreting data.	NO	IP	FP	CP	CTO
11. Participates with others in shared governance processes that integrate data into decision making.	NO	IP	FP	CP	CTO
Total numbers	—	—	—	—	—

Note: NO = not observed; IP = infrequently performed; F = frequently performed; CP = consistently performed; CTO = can teach to others.

D. Roles and responsibilities that reflect broad involvement and collaboration

12. Own role includes attention to the classroom, the school, the community, and the profession.	NO	IP	FP	CP	CTO
13. Observes and is sensitive to indicators that participants are performing outside traditional roles. Gives feedback to participants regarding the benefit of these changes.	NO	IP	FP	CP	CTO
14. Develops strategies for strengthening the new relationships that will emerge from broadened roles.	NO	IP	FP	CP	CTO
15. Develops mutual expectations and strategies for ensuring that participants share responsibility for the implementation of school community agreements.	NO	IP	FP	CP	CTO
Total numbers	—	—	—	—	—

E. Reflective practice/innovation as the norm

16. Ensures that the cycle of inquiry and time schedules involve a continuous and ongoing reflective phase.	NO	IP	FP	CP	CTO
17. Demonstrates and encourages individual and group initiative by providing access to resources, personnel, time, and outside networks.	NO	IP	FP	CP	CTO
18. Practices and supports innovation without expectations for early success.	NO	IP	FP	CP	CTO
19. Encourages and participates in collaborative innovation.	NO	IP	FP	CP	CTO

Note: NO = not observed; IP = infrequently performed; F = frequently performed; CP = consistently performed; CTO = can teach to others.

E. Reflective practice/innovation as the norm—continued

	NO	IP	FP	CP	CTO
20. Engages with other innovators in developing own criteria for monitoring, assessment, and accountability regrading own individual and shared work.	NO	IP	FP	CP	CTO
Total numbers	—	—	—	—	—

F. High student achievement

	NO	IP	FP	CP	CTO
21. Works with members of the school community to establish challenging and human expectations and standards.	NO	IP	FP	CP	CTO
22. Designs, teaches, coaches, and assesses authentic curriculum, instruction, and performance-based assessment processes that ensure that all children learn.	NO	IP	FP	CP	CTO
23. Provides systematic feedback to children and families about student progress.	NO	IP	FP	CP	CTO
24. Receives feedback about family learning expectations.	NO	IP	FP	CP	CTO
25. Redesigns roles and structures to enable the school to develop and sustain resiliency in children (e.g., teacher as coach/counselor/mentor).	NO	IP	FP	CP	CTO
26. Ensures that the learning cycle within the school includes evidence from performance-based assessment, examination of student work, and research.	NO	IP	FP	CP	CTO
Total numbers	—	—	—	—	—

Note: NO = not observed; IP = infrequently performed; F = frequently performed; CP = consistently performed; CTO = can teach to others.

Scoring: Summarize the number of responses in each category of characteristics in three broad groups: NO/IP, FP/CP, and CTO.

	NO/IP	FP/CP	CTO
A: Broad-based participation in the work of leadership			
B: Skillful participation in the work of leadership			
C: Inquiry-based use of information to inform shared decisions and practice			
D: Roles and responsibilities that reflect broad involvement and collaboration			
E: Reflective practice/innovation as the norm			
F: High student achievement			

Suggestion: Note each area (A–F) in your professional development plans; identify specific dispositions and skills in category or group: NO/IP, FP/CP, and CTO. Suggested learning plan:

NO/IP areas: Find opportunities to observe these behaviors; participate in specific training.

FP/CP areas: Find more opportunities to demonstrate and practice.

CTO areas: Find opportunities to teach and coach others; participate in formal governance groups.

LEADERSHIP CAPACITY
SCHOOL SURVEY

This school survey is designed to assess the leadership capacity conditions that exist in your school. The items are clustered by the characteristics of schools with high leadership capacity. After each staff member has completed this survey and totaled the results, this information can be presented in a chart that depicts schoolwide needs. Beside each item is a Likert-type scale:

1 = We do not do this in our school.

2 = We are starting to move in this direction.

3 = We are making good progress here.

4 = We have this condition well established.

5 = We are refining our practice in this area.

Circle the most appropriate number.

A. Broad-based, skillful participation in the work of leadership

In our school, we . . . .

1. have established representative governance groups;	1	2	3	4	5
2. perform collaborative work in large and small groups;	1	2	3	4	5
3. model and demonstrate leadership skills;	1	2	3	4	5
4. organize for maximum interaction among adults and children;	1	2	3	4	5
5. share authority and resources;	1	2	3	4	5
6. express our leadership by attending to the learning of the entire school community;	1	2	3	4	5
7. engage each other in these opportunities to lead.	1	2	3	4	5
TOTAL (add circled numbers, down and then across columns) _____ =					

B. Inquiry-based use of information to inform shared decisions and practice

In our school, we . . . .

8. use a learning cycle that involves reflection, dialogue, inquiry, construction of new meanings and action;	1	2	3	4	5
9. make time available for this learning to occur (e.g., faculty meetings, ad hoc groups, teams);	1	2	3	4	5

Note: 1 = We do not do this in our school; 2 = We are starting to move in this direction; 3 = We are making good progress here; 4 = We have this condition well established; 5 = We are refining our practice in this area.

B. Inquiry-based use of information to inform shared decisions and practice—continued

	1	2	3	4	5
10. connect our learning cycles to our highest priorities, our teaching and learning purposes;	1	2	3	4	5
11. identify, discover, and interpret information and data/evidence that are used to inform our decisions and teaching practices;	1	2	3	4	5
12. have designed a comprehensive information system that keeps everyone informed and involved.	1	2	3	4	5
TOTAL (add circled numbers, down and then across columns) ____ = ____					

C. Roles and responsibilities that reflect broad involvement and collaboration

In our school, we . . .

	1	2	3	4	5
13. have designed our roles to include attention to our classrooms, the school, the community, and the profession;	1	2	3	4	5
14. are sensitive to indications that we are performing outside of traditional roles;	1	2	3	4	5
15. have developed new ways in which we can work together to nurture our relationships with each other;	1	2	3	4	5
16. have developed a plan for shared responsibilities in the implementation of our decisions and agreements.	1	2	3	4	5
TOTAL (add circled numbers, down and then across columns) ____ = ____					

Note: 1 = We do not do this in our school; 2 = We are starting to move in this direction; 3 = We are making good progress here; 4 = We have this condition well established; 5 = We are refining our practice in this area.

D. Reflective practice/innovation as the norm

In our school, we . . . .

17. make sure that the learning cycle and time schedules include times and places for continuous and ongoing reflection;	1	2	3	4	5
18. demonstrate and encourage individual and group initiative by providing access to resources, personnel, and time;	1	2	3	4	5
19. have joined with networks of other schools and programs, both inside and outside the district, to secure feedback on our work;	1	2	3	4	5
20. practice and support innovation without unrealistic expectations of early success;	1	2	3	4	5
21. encourage and participate in collaborative innovations;	1	2	3	4	5
22. develop our own criteria for monitoring, assessment, and accountability regarding our individual and shared work.	1	2	3	4	5
TOTAL (add circled numbers, down and then across columns) _____ = _____					

E. High student achievement

In our school, we . . . .

23. work with members of the school community to establish challenging and humane expectations and standards;	1	2	3	4	5

Note: 1 = We do not do this in our school; 2 = We are starting to move in this direction; 3 = We are making good progress here; 4 = We have this condition well established; 5 = We are refining our practice in this area.

E. High student achievement—continued

24. design, teach, coach, and assess authentic curriculum, instruction, and performance-based assessment processes that insure that all children learn;	1	2	3	4	5
25. provide systematic feedback to children and families about student progress;	1	2	3	4	5
26. receive feedback from families about student performance and school programs;	1	2	3	4	5
27. have redesigned roles and structures to develop and sustain resiliency in children (e.g., teacher as coach/advisor/mentor, schoolwide guidance programs, community service).	1	2	3	4	5
TOTAL (add circled numbers, down and then across columns) ——— = ———					

Comments, perceptions, insights that you want to remember:

Note: 1 = We do not do this in our school; 2 = We are starting to move in this direction; 3 = We are making good progress here; 4 = We have this condition well established; 5 = We are refining our practice in this area.

School scoring. Add staff totals for each area, A to E. Possible scores can be found by multiplying the number possible for each category by the number of staff completing the survey (see column "Possible Scores" in the following table). List the "School Totals" from the following table on chart paper for all to see. The areas that received the lowest numbers are the areas of greatest need. Discuss each area, distinguishing among items in order to identify areas of growth. Columns 1 and 2 in the survey represent areas of greatest need. Columns 3 and 4 represent strengths. Column 5 represents exemplary work as a school with high leadership capacity. Select areas to address in your school planning.

Characteristics	School Totals	Possible Scores
A. Broad-based participation in the work of leadership		35x = ___
B. Inquiry-based use of information to inform shared decisions and practice		25x = ___
C. Roles and responsibilities that reflect broad involvement and collaboration		20x = ___
D. Reflective practice/innovation as the norm		20x = ___
E. High student achievement		25x = ___

Note: In Column 3, x = no. of staff completing survey.

Appendix C

Rubric of Emerging Teacher Leadership

From ⎯⎯⎯⎯⎯⎯⎯⎯⎯⎯⎯⎯⎯⎯⎯⎯⎯⟶ To

A. Adult Development

1. Defines self in relation to others in the community. The opinions of others, particularly those in authority, are highly important.	Defines self as independent from the group, separating needs and goals from others. Does not often see the need for group action.	Understands self as interdependent with others in the school community, seeking feedback from others and counsel from self.	Engages colleagues in acting out of a *sense of self* and shared values, forming interdependent learning communities.

Note: This rubric was developed in 1995 by Linda Lambert, Director of the Center for Educational Leadership at the University of California–Hayward, in cooperation with K–12 educators, graduate students, and faculty.

From ⎯⎯⎯⎯⎯⎯⟶ To

A. Adult Development—continued

2. Does not yet recognize the need for self-reflection. Tends to implement strategies as learned without making adjustments arising from reflective practice.	Personal reflection leads to refinement of strategies and routines. Does not often share reflections with others. Focuses on argument for own ideas. Does not support systems that are designed to enhance reflective practice.	Engages in self-reflection as a means of improving practices. Models these processes for others in the school community. Holds conversations that share views and develops understanding of each other's assumptions.	Evokes reflection in others. Develops and supports a culture for *self-reflection* that may include collaborative planning, peer coaching, action research, and reflective writing.
3. Absence of ongoing evaluation of own teaching. Does not yet systematically connect teacher and student behaviors.	Self-evaluation is not often shared with others; however, responsibility for problems or errors is typically ascribed to others such as students or family.	Highly self-evaluative and introspective. Accepts shared responsibility as a natural part of a school community. No need for blame.	Enables others to be *self-evaluative* and introspective, leading toward self- and shared *responsibility.*

From ——————————————> To

A. Adult Development—continued

From		To
4. In need of effective strategies to demonstrate respect and concern for others. Is polite and congenial, yet primarily focuses on own needs.	Exhibits respectful attitude toward others in most situations, usually privately. Can be disrespectful in public debate. Gives little feedback to others.	Consistently shows respect and concern for all members of the school community. Validates and respects qualities in and opinions of others.	Encourages and supports others in being *respectful, caring, trusted members of the school community.* Initiates recognition of the ideas and achievements of colleagues as part of an overall goal of collegial empowerment

B. Dialogue

From		To
5. Interactions with others are primarily social, not based on shared goals or group learning.	Communicates with others around logistical issues/problems. Sees goals as individually set for each classroom, not actively participating in efforts to focus on common goals.	Communicates well with individuals and groups in the community as a means of creating and sustaining relationships and focusing on teaching and learning. Actively participates in dialogue.	*Facilitates effective dialogue* among members of the school community in order to build relationships and focus the dialogue on teaching and learning.

From ——————> To

B. Dialogue—continued

From		> To
6. Does not pose questions of or seek to influence the group. Participation often resembles consent or compliance.	Makes personal point of view, although not assumptions, explicit. When opposed to ideas, often asks impeding questions that can derail or divert the dialogue.	Asks questions and provides insights that reflect an understanding of the need to surface assumptions and address the goals of the community.	Facilitates communica-tion among colleagues by asking *provocative or facilitative questions* that open productive dialogue.
7. Does not actively seek information or new professional knowledge that challenges current practices. Shares knowledge with others only when requested.	Attends registered staff development activities that are planned by the school or district. Occasionally shares knowledge during formal and informal gatherings. Does not seek knowledge that challenges status quo.	Possesses current knowledge and information about teaching and learning. Actively seeks to use that understanding to alter teaching practices. Studies own practice.	Works with others to *construct knowledge through multiple forms of inquiry,* action research, examina-tion of disaggregated school data, insights from others and from the outside research community.

From ——————>	To

B. Dialogue—continued

8. Responds to situations in similar ways; expects predictable responses from others. Is sometimes confused by variations from expected norms.	Responds to situations in different though predictable ways. Expects consistency from those in authority and from self.	Responds to situations with open-mindedness and flexibility; welcomes multiple perspectives from others. Alters own assumptions during dialogue when evidence is persuasive.	Promotes *open-mindedness and flexibility* in others; invites multiple perspectives and interpretations as a means of challenging old assumptions and framing new actions.

C. Collaboration

9. Decision making is based on individual wants and needs rather than those of the group as a whole.	Promotes individual autonomy in classroom decision making. Relegates school decision making to the principal.	Actively participates in shared decision making. Volunteers to follow through on group decisions.	Promotes *collaborative decision making* that provides options to meet the diverse individual and group needs of the school community.

From ——————————————————> To

C. Collaboration—continued

From			To
10. Sees little value in team building, although seeks membership in the group. Will participate, but may not connect activities with larger school goals.	Does not seek to participate in roles or settings that would involve team building. Considers most team-building activities to be pate "touchy-feely" and frivolous.	Is an active participant in team building, seeking roles and opportunities to contribute to the work of the team. Sees "teamness" as central to community.	Engages colleagues in *team-building activities* that develop mutual trust, and promotes collaborative decision making.
11. Sees problems as caused by the actions of others, e.g., students or parents; or blames self. Uncertain regarding the specifics of own involvement.	Interprets problems from own perspective. Plays the role of observer and critic, not accepting responsibility for emerging issues and dilemmas. Considers most problems to be a function of poor management.	Acknowledges that problems involve all members of the community. Actively seeks to define problems and proposes resolutions or approaches that address the situation. Finding blame is not relevant.	Engages colleagues in identifying and acknowledging problems. Acts with others to *frame problems and seek resolutions.* Anticipates situations that may cause recurrent problems.

From ⎯⎯⎯⎯⎯⎯⎯⟶ To

C. Collaboration—continued

12. Does not recognize or avoids conflict in the school community. Misdirects frustrations into withdrawal or personal hurt. Avoids talking about issues that could evoke conflict.	Does not shy away from conflict. Engages conflict as a means of surfacing competing ideas, approaches. Understands that conflict is intimidating to many.	Anticipates and seeks to resolve or intervene in conflict. Actively tries to channel conflict into problem-solving endeavors. Is not intimidated by conflict, although would not seek it.	*Surfaces, addresses, and mediates conflict* within the school and with parents and community. Understands that negotiating conflict is necessary for personal and school change.

D. Organizational Change

13. Focuses on present situations and issues; seldom plans for either short- or long-term futures. Expects certainty.	Demonstrates forward thinking in some curriculum for own classroom. Usually does not connect own planning to the future of the school.	Develops forward-thinking skills in working with others and planning for school improvements. Future goals based on shared values and vision.	Provides for and creates opportunities to engage others in *forward (visionary) thinking and planning* based on shared core values.

From ———————————————⟶ To

D. Organizational Change—continued

14. Maintains a low profile during school change, basically uninvolved in group processes. Attempts to comply with changes. Expects compliance from others.	Questions status quo; suggests that others need to change to reestablish the "good old days." Selects those changes that reflect personal philosophies. Opposes or ignores practices that require a schoolwide focus.	Shows enthusiasm and involvement in school change. Leads by example. Explores possibilities and implements changes for both personal and professional development.	Initiates *actions toward innovative change;* motivates and draws others into the action for school and district improvements. Encourages others to *implement practices that support schoolwide learning.* Provides follow-up planning and coaching support.

From ——————> To

D. Organizational Change—continued

From		To
15. Culturally unaware. "I treat everyone the same." Stage of naivete to sociopolitical implications of race, culture, ethnic, and gender issues.	Growing sensitivity to political implications of diversity. Acknowledges that cultural differences exist and influence individuals and organizations.	Acceptance and understanding; "aha" level. Has developed an appreciation of own cultural identities and a deeper appreciation/ respect for cultural differences. Applies understanding in classroom and school.	Commitment to value of and building on *cultural differences*. Actively seeks to involve others in designing programs and policies that support the development of a multicultural world.
16. Attends to students in his or her own classroom. Possessive of children and space. Has not yet secured a developmental view of children.	Concerned for the preparation of children in previous grades. Critical of preparation of children and readiness of children to meet established standards.	Developmental view of children translates into concern for all children in the school (not only those in own classroom) and their future performances in later educational settings.	Works with colleagues to develop programs and policies that take *wholistic view of children's development* (e.g., multigraded classrooms, multiyear teacher assignments, parent education, follow-up studies).

From ⟶ To

D. Organizational Change—continued

17. Works alongside new teachers. Is cordial although does not offer assistance. Lacks confidence in giving feedback to others.	Shares limited information with new teachers, mainly information that pertains to administrative functions in the school (e.g., attendance accounting, grade reports). Does not offer to serve as a master teacher.	Collaborates with, supports, and gives feedback to new and student teachers. Often serves as master or cooperating teacher.	*Takes responsibility for the support and development of systems for new and student teachers.* Develops collaborative programs with school, district, and universities.
18. Displays little interest in the selection of new teachers. Assumes that they will be appointed by the district or those otherwise in authority.	Assumes that district will recruit and appoint teachers. Has not proposed a more active role to the teachers association.	Becomes actively involved in the setting of criteria and the selection of new teachers.	Advocates to the schools, district, and teachers association the *development of hiring practices* that involve teachers, parents, and students in the processes. *Promotes the hiring of diverse candidates.*

SCHOOL DISTRICT PERSONNEL PRACTICES AND POLICIES

Traditional/Hierarchical/ Centralized	Collaborative/Constructivist/ Decentralized
Selection of Personnel	
Paper screening followed by broad-based interview panel; occasional teaching/supervision sample or observed performance; site visitations for administrative positions; final selection by central authority.	Augmented by mini-assessment center featuring authentic simulations, interactive role playing, problem-solving exercises, personal valuing of dilemmas (with teachers trained to serve as assessors); major authority for selection at the site, with broad-based participation in the process.
Induction of New Personnel	
Formal orientation activities, followed by standardized staff development programs; may include access to a mentor; usually self-contained and not sustained.	Orientation and enculturation processes for both teachers and administrators include formal and informal activities that are part of a complex professional development program. Strong links with local universities, regional and county offices, other districts, professional networks. Professional practice schools as exemplary model.

Traditional/Hierarchical/ Centralized	Collaborative/Constructivist/ Decentralized

Professional Development

Emphasis on skill development, knowledge acquisition, training by prescription; delivery through formal workshops, courses.	Emphasis on professional development as multiple learning opportunities embedded in authentic tasks such as collaborative action research, study groups, participation in decision making, coplanning, mentoring of new educators.
Individual professional development plans, where they exist, are objective-based in relation to teacher evaluation criteria and are determined by evaluator.	Professional development plans are personalized, collegial, and school-based, with room for choice, sustained commitment, and multiple forms of learning.
Majority of professional development days are scheduled and structured by the district and/or board.	Majority of professional development days are designed by local staff who are also involved in determining district priorities that shape the common days and programs. Programs feature work in reciprocal processes, action research, teaching and learning from student work, leadership team development, protocols, reciprocal team coaching, collaborative planning.

Traditional/Hierarchical/ Centralized	Collaborative/Constructivist/ Decentralized

Professional Development—continued

District goals dominate the design of local school improvement plans. School plans are viewed primarily as instrumental in moving towards district goals.	Local school improvement plans have ongoing professional development at the center. School plans inform as well as are informed by district goals.

Reassignment and Transfer

Contract provisions and the "needs of the district" control matters of assignment and transfer. Often, poorly performing staff are transferred from school to school.	Reassignment is requested by an educator attracted to the program and philosophy of another school; educator is invited to another school because of needed skills and perspective.

Supervision and Evaluation

Supervision is performed by administrators and quasi-administrators, such as department chairs. Peer coaching and informal supervision may be encouraged, but the enabling structures for sustained collegial work do not exist.	Critical self-analysis, peer observation and feedback, cognitive coaching, critical friendship, engagement in collaborative action research. These norms constitute the core of collegial "supervision" and evaluation practice.

Traditional/Hierarchical/ Centralized	Collaborative/Constructivist/ Decentralized

Supervision and Evaluation—continued

Evaluation is performed only by administrators and in strict compliance with contract and district effectiveness criteria. Number of allowable observations often limited by contract.

Administrators participate in evaluation (especially with new teachers and those experiencing difficulty), but their assessments simply add to a performance portfolio which also includes self- and peer assessment reports, student and parent feedback, research findings, and other performance artifacts.

Contracts, Regulations, and Waivers

Adversarial contract negotiations and centrally designed policies and regulations.

Nonconfrontational, interest-based bargaining produces contracts that are congruent with flexible district policies.

Emphasis is placed on developing clear, detailed, and replicable clauses, regulations, and procedures for compliance.

Policies and procedures parameters serve emerging goals; flexible policies grow out of change efforts and respond to needs identified by school-site leadership teams.

Exemptions and waiver procedures may be made available, but they are viewed as evidences of weakness or failure.

Waivers to state department and legal regulations are framed and supported by district as such waivers respond to local changes.

Source: The Constructivist Leader (pp. 149–150), by L. Lambert, D. Walker, D. Zimmerman, J. Cooper, M. D. Lambert, M. E. Gardner, & P. J. Ford-Slack (1995). New York: Teachers College Press. Reproduced by permission of Teachers College Press.

REFERENCES

Calhoun, E. (1994). *How to use action research in the self-renewing school.* Alexandria, VA: ASCD.

Costa, A. L., & Garmston, R. J. (1994). *Cognitive coaching: A foundation for renaissance schools.* Norwood, MA: Christopher-Gordon Publishers.

Darling-Hammond, L. (1993). Reframing the school reform agenda: Developing capacity for school transformation. *Phi Delta Kappan, 74*(10), 752–761.

Evans, R. (1996). *The human side of school change.* San Francisco: Jossey-Bass.

Glickman, C. (1993). *Renewing America's schools: A guide for school-based action.* San Francisco: Jossey-Bass.

Lambert, L., Kent, K., Richert, A. E., Collay, M., & Dietz, M. E. (1997). *Who will save our schools? Teachers as constructivist leaders.* Thousand Oaks, CA: Corwin Press.

Lambert, L., Walker, D., Zimmerman, D., Cooper, J., Lambert, M. D., Gardner, M. E., & Ford-Slack, P. J. (1995). *The constructivist leader.* New York: Teachers College Press.

Lieberman, A. (Ed.). (1995). *The work of restructuring schools: Building from the ground up.* New York: Teachers College Press.

Louis, K. S. (1989). The role of the school district in school improvement. In M. Holmes, K. Leithwood, & D. Musella (Eds.), *Educational policy for effective schools* (pp. 145–167). Toronto: Ontario Institute for Studies in Education Press.

McDonald, J. P. (1996). *Redesigning school: Lessons for the 21st century.* San Francisco: Jossey-Bass.

Newmann, F. M., & Wehlage, G. G. (1995). *Successful school restructuring: A report to the public and educators by the Center on Organization and Restructuring of Schools*. Madison, WI: Center on Organization and Restructuring of Schools.

Sagor, R. (1992). *How to conduct collaborative action research*. Alexandria, VA: ASCD.

BIBLIOGRAPHY

Aburto, S., & Kim, Y. (1992, April). *Comparing superintendents', title VII directors', and school principals' perceptions of capacity building success*. Paper presented at the annual meeting of the American Educational Research Association, San Francisco.

Calhoun, E. (1994). *How to use action research in the self-renewing school*. Alexandria, VA: ASCD.

Canady, R. L., & Retting, M. D. (Eds.). (1996). *Teaching in the block*. Larchmont, NY: Eye on Education.

Capra, F. (1996). *The web of life*. New York: Doubleday.

Carnegie Council for Adolescent Development. (1989). *Turning points*. Washington, DC: Author.

Center on Organization and Restructuring of Schools. (1994). *Effects of high school restructuring and size on gains in achievement and engagement for early secondary school students*. Madison, WI: Author.

Center on Organization and Restructuring of Schools. (1995). *Understanding high school restructuring effects on the equitable distribution of learning in mathematics and science*. Madison, WI: Author.

Clifford, R. M. (1990, November). *Professional development as a form of capacity building*. Paper presented at the Conference on Preparation and Professional Development Programs for Early Childhood Educators, New York.

Costa, A. L., & Garmston, R. J. (1994). *Cognitive coaching: A foundation for renaissance schools*. Norwood, MA: Christopher-Gordon Publishers.

Darling-Hammond, L. (1993). Reframing the school reform agenda: Developing capacity for school transformation. *Phi Delta Kappan*, 74(10), 752–761.

Darling-Hammond, L., Ancess, J., & Falk, B. (1995). *Authentic assessment in action: Studies of schools and students at work*. New York: Teachers College Press.

Davidson, B. M., & Dell, G. L. (1994, April). *Building capacity for educational change: A portrait of behavioral patterns of first year schools in the Louisiana Accelerated Schools Network*. Paper presented at the annual meeting of the American Educational Research Association, New Orleans, LA.

Evans, R. (1996). *The human side of school change*. San Francisco: Jossey-Bass.

Finnan, C. (Ed.). (1996). *Accelerated schools in action: Lessons from the field*. Thousand Oaks, CA: Corwin Press.

Floden, R. E., Goertz, M. E., & O'Day, J. (1995, September). Capacity building in systemic reform. *Phi Delta Kappan*, 77(1), 19–21.

Fuhrman, S. H. (1994). *Challenges in systemic education reform: CPRE policy briefs*. New Brunswick, NJ: Consortium for Policy Research in Education.

Glickman, C. (1993). *Renewing America's schools: A guide for school-based action*. San Francisco: Jossey-Bass.

Heifetz, R. A. (1995). *Leadership without easy answers*. Cambridge, MA: The Belknap Press of Harvard University Press.

Henderson, N., & Milstein, M. (1996). *Resiliency in schools*. Thousand Oaks, CA: Corwin Press.

Kyle, R. (1993). *Transforming our schools: Lessons from the Jefferson County Public Schools/Gheens Professional Development Academy 1983–91*. Louisville, KY: Gheens Foundation.

Lambert, L. (1997). *Student achievement and school restructuring factors: A significant research base*. Hayward: California State University.

Lambert, L., Kent, K., Richert, A. E., Collay, M., & Dietz, M. E. (1997). *Who will save our schools? Teachers as constructivist leaders*. Thousand Oaks, CA: Corwin Press.

Lambert, L., Walker, D., Zimmerman, D., Cooper, J., Lambert, M. D., Gardner, M. E., & Ford-Slack, P. J. (1995). *The constructivist leader*. New York: Teachers College Press.

Lee, V. E., Bryk, A. S., & Smith, J. B. (1993). The organization of effective secondary schools. In L. Darling-Hammond (Ed.), *Review of Research in Education, 19*, 171–267.

Lee, V. E., & Smith, J. B. (1994). High school restructuring and student achievement: A new study finds strong links. *Issues in Restructuring Schools, 7,* 1–5, 16.

Lieberman, A. (Ed.). (1995). *The work of restructuring schools: Building from the ground up.* New York: Teachers College Press.

Louis, K. S. (1989). The role of the school district in school improvement. In M. Holmes, K. Leithwood, & D. Musella (Eds.), *Educational policy for effective schools* (pp. 145–167). Toronto: Ontario Institute for Studies in Education Press.

Luther, J. (1994, July). The learning community: Survival and sustainability on the plains. In *Issues affecting rural communities.* Proceedings of an International Conference held by the Rural Education Research and Development Centre, Townsville, Queensland, Australia.

MacMullen, M. (1996). The Coalition of Essential Schools: A national research context [Appendix B]. In T. Sizer, *Horace's Hope.* New York: Houghton-Mifflin.

McDonald, J. P. (1996). *Redesigning school: Lessons for the 21st century.* San Francisco: Jossey Bass.

National Association of Secondary School Principals. (1996). *Breaking ranks: Changing an American institution. A report on the high school of the 21st century.* Reston, VA: Author.

Newmann, F. M., & Wehlage, G. G. (1995). *Successful school restructuring: A report to the public and educators by the Center on Organization and Restructuring of Schools.* Madison, WI: Center on Organization and Restructuring of Schools.

Office of Educational Research and Improvement. (1993). *Building capacity for systemic reform.* (Report No. PIP-93-1505). Washington, DC: Programs for the Improvement of Practice, U.S. Department of Education.

Sagor, R. (1992). *How to conduct collaborative action research.* Alexandria, VA: ASCD.

Schmoker, M. (1996). *Results: The key to continuous school improvement.* Alexandria, VA: ASCD.

Shields, P. M. (1995). *Improving schools from the bottom up: From effective schools to restructuring* (Final report). Menlo Park, CA: Stanford Research Institute International.

Wasley, P., Hampel, R., & Clark, R. (1997). The puzzle of whole-school change. *Phi Delta Kappan, 78*(9), 690–697.

INDEX

About the Author

Linda Lambert is a Professor at California State University-Hayward (CSUH). In her current role she works with administrative candidates and their schools, particularly in the urban Bay Area, as well as in schools and agencies throughout the United States. Before joining the faculty at CSUH, Lambert was a teacher leader, principal, district and county professional development director, coordinator of a Principals' Center and Leadership Academy, and designer of four major restructuring programs.

From 1989 to 1993, she worked in Egypt to set up a National Curriculum Center, and in Thailand and Mexico in leadership development. The lead author of *The Constructivist Leader* (1995) and *Who Will Save Our Schools: Teachers as Constructivist Leaders* (1997), she has also written numerous articles and chapters in her fields of interest. Her research and consultancy interests include leadership, professional and organizational development, and school and district restructuring.

Linda and her husband, Morgan, have 6 children and 10 grandchildren and live in Oakland, California. You may reach her at CSUH, Hayward, CA 94542-3080 USA (E-mail: Linlambert@aol.com).